Networking for Beginners

Be Familiar with Computer Network Basics. Learn What a Computer Network is, Why It Matters and How Networking May Raise a Challenge to Machine Learning.

Scott Chesterton

Table of Contents

Introduction

Congratulations on downloading *Networking for beginners* and thank you for doing so.

The following chapters will discuss the basics of computer networking and its protocols in a clear crystal detail in a way such that you will be able to understand them easily in very less time.

Computer networking is the greatest invention mankind has ever seen due to its vast opportunities and great technologies that had made human life luxurious and had paved a way for the greatest knowledge transfer we could ever think of.

This book deals with computer networking in layman terms in a way such that newbies can appreciate the complex process that deals with computer networking. TCP/IP a famous network protocol is also described in detail for better understanding of the various protocols that are essential for good network communication.

Machine learning is a phenomenon in the tech industry which is efficient and accurate. Networking for beginners explains how machine learning can be interlinked with computer networks for better network security and thus a better Internet away from malicious hackers.

There are plenty of books on this subject on the market, thanks again for choosing this one! Every effort was made to ensure it is full of as much useful information as possible, please enjoy!

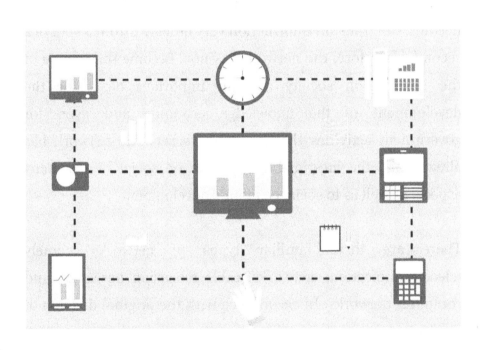

Chapter 1: Introducing Computer Networking

We know that some of the 21st century's important characteristics are digital, network, and information, these had made the world a better place to live. In order to realize information, we must rely on a perfect network, because the network can transmit information very quickly within a split of a second. Therefore, the network has now become the lifeline of the information society and an important basis for the development of the knowledge economy and even for government activities that go on in secret. The network has already had the inestimable influence on social life in many aspects as well as to social economic development.

There are three familiar types of networks namely telecommunications networks, cable television networks, and computer networks. In accordance with the original division of services, telecommunications networks provide users with telephone, telegraph and fax services. Cable television delivers a variety of TV shows to its users. Computer networks enable users to transfer data files between computers. These three kinds of networks all play a very important role in the information process, but among them, the fastest development and which plays a central role is the computer network.

With the development of technology, the telecommunication network and the cable television network have gradually integrated into the technology of the modern computer network for example as Skype and Netflix, expanding the original service range of they intended to be. But the computer network also can provide telephone communication, video communication as well as the transmission video program service to the user. In theory, the above three networks can be integrated into a network to provide all the above services but however, it is often not possible.

Since the 1990s, the computer network represented by the Internet has developed rapidly, from the free education and Scientific Research Network for Americans to the Commercial Network for global use as the largest computer network in the world. Computer networks have only been around for more than 50 years (the real computer networks began with the creation of ARPAnet by the Defense Advanced Research Projects Agency (ARPA) in 1969, which is described later in this book). In this short time of 50 years, the development and popularization of computer network technology in various fields really can be described as a phenomenal journey. It's really hard to imagine that the first-gigabit connection rates have grown to tens of gigabits in such a short period of time, increasing by thousands of times. With the development of computer network technology and its scope, the advantages and applications of the computer network are unimaginable. Before talking about applications of computer network let us discuss briefly the definition of a computer network.

The term information and Communication Society has become synonymous with the modern world. People can use mobile phones and other information terminals at any time to communicate anywhere, and this environment is dependent on the network to achieve.

However, with the development and popularization of the Internet, many new challenges have emerged. In order to transmit a large amount of data in an instant and efficiently, it is necessary to study how to construct a complex network. Even more, it is necessary to consider how to carry out strict routing control in such a complex network. In order to overcome these challenges, efforts are being made to improve the cost-effectiveness of network construction, to update network equipment according to market requirements, and to develop better maintenance tools for the stable operation of complex networks. At the same time, efforts are being made to train a group of capable network technicians as soon as possible.

The computer is having an inestimable influence on our society and life. Today, the computer has been used in a variety of fields, so that some people say "the greatest invention of the 20th century is the computer. ". Computers have been introduced not only into offices, factories, schools, educational institutions, and laboratories but also into personal computers at home. At the same time, the number of people who own portable devices such as laptops, tablets and mobile phone terminals (smartphones) is growing Even devices that look nothing like computers, such as home appliances, music players, office appliances, and cars, typically have a small chip built into them to give them the computer control they need. Inadvertently, our working life has been closely linked to the computer. And most of the computers we use and devices with built-in computers are networked.

In the beginning, computers were widely used in stand-alone mode. However, with the continuous development of computers, people are no longer confined to the single-computer model but will be connected to a computer network. By connecting multiple computers, information can be shared and information can be transferred between two machines located far away from each other. Initially, a network of computers is formed by administrators connecting specific computers together. For example, the connection of computers held by the same company or laboratory or the connection of computers between businesses doing business with one another. All in all, it's a private network. With the development of this kind of private network, people begin to try to connect several private networks to form a larger private network. This network gradually evolved into the Internet for public use.

When connected to the Internet, computer-to-computer communication is no longer confined to companies or departments but can communicate with any computer on the Internet. The Internet, as a new technology, greatly enriched the means of communication of telephone, post, and fax, and was gradually accepted by people.

Since then, people have been developing various Internet access technologies, enabling various kinds of communication terminals to connect to the Internet, making the Internet A world-class computer network to create the integrated communications environment we have today.

A computer network is like a person's nervous system. All the senses in a person's body are transmitted to the brain via nerves. Similarly, information from around the world is delivered to everyone's computer via the web. With the explosive development and popularization of the Internet, information networks have been everywhere. Community members, school students can be through the mail group (using e-mail Bulletin Board functions. All members who subscribe to the mail group can receive mail sent to the group.), The home page, BBS forum contact each other, it can even be accessed via a weblog (A text-centric home page or service. Users can update content as easy as keeping a diary.), Chat Rooms, instant messaging, and SNS (social networks). A network of individuals or groups on the Internet. Through SNS, people can publish their recent activities, life feelings and the latest works, so that members of the circle real-time personal dynamic.

Definition of Computer Network

A computer network is made up primarily of interconnecting common, programmable hardware. The hardware is designed for a specific purpose (for example, to transmit data or video signals). This programmable hardware can be used to transmit a variety of different types of data and can support a wide and growing range of applications.

According to this definition: (1) the hardware connected to a computer network is not limited to ordinary computers, but includes smartphones and other different types of devices like AR devices, smartwatches that are flooding the market every day (2) computer networks are not specifically designed to transmit data, but are capable of supporting a wide variety of applications (including those that may arise in the future).

We know that in the beginning, computer networks were really used to transmit data. But with the development of network technology, the application scope of a computer network is increasing, not only networks can transmit audio and video files, but also the application scope has far exceeded the general communication scope and can be perfectly used for many applications.

It is generally believed that computer network refers to the connection of multiple computers and network equipment with independent instruments in different geographical locations through communication lines (including transmission media and network equipment). A computer system for resource sharing and information transfer under the co-management and coordination of Network Operating System, network management software and network communication protocol. If you don't know what a computer network is, go home, or go to an Internet cafe, or go to your company and see for yourself. What you see is a network of pcs (personal computers) that appear to be independent and located in different places, connected by cables and boxes of devices (switches, routers).

Simply put, a computer network is a collection of computer systems, or groups of computer systems, that work independently and are connected to each other by communication lines, including connecting cables and network equipment. In this set of computer systems, resources can be shared among computers, access to each other can be carried out for a variety of computer network applications. The computers can be microcomputers, minicomputers, midsized computers, mainframes.

By sharing, I mean sharing resources. Resource sharing has many implications. It can be information sharing, software sharing, or hardware sharing. For example, there are many servers on the Internet (that is, a dedicated computer) that store a large number of valuable electronic documents (including audio and video files) that can be easily read or downloaded (for free or for a fee) by Internet users. Because of the network, these resources are as easy to use as if they were right next to the user.

A typical example of data resource sharing is database resource sharing, where each network user can centrally invoke relevant data information in a single database server. A variety of application servers are also examples of sharing data resources, such as receiving email through client-side programs like Fox Mail and Outlook, and the online games you and your friends play every day Or you and your Family Watch the same movie on the Internet every day on a different computer at home. There are many examples of sharing software resources, such as in the enterprise internal network we will provide all employees on the server to share some common tools, let users choose to install. If pushed to the Internet, it is more intuitive, we downloaded from the Internet are all examples of software resource sharing.

Now we will discuss different types of computer networks and how they are divided based on certain categories.

Categorized by the Scope of the Network

The Wide Area Network (Wan)

This is the core part of the Internet, and its mission is to transport data sent by hosts over long distances (across different countries, for example) . The links connecting the switches of Wan nodes are usually high-speed links with large communication capacity.

Metropolitan Area Network (Man)

The scope of Metropolitan Area Network (MAN) is generally a city, can span several blocks or even the whole city, the distance of its function is about 5 ~ 50 km. A Metropolitan Area Network can be owned by one or more units, but it can also be a utility used to interconnect multiple LANs that is local area networks. At present, many metropolitan area networks (Man) are based on Ethernet technology.

Local Area Network (LAN) In the early days of Lan Development, a school or factory often had only one Lan, but now the LAN is widely used for different purposes. Most schools or businesses have many interconnected LANs (such networks are often called campus networks, or corporate networks).

Personal Area Network (Pan)

A Personal Area Network (Pan) is a Network that connects Personal electronic devices (such as portable computers) for Personal use wirelessly at a person's place of work or home. This is often referred to as a Wireless personal area network (WPAN), which has a small range of about 10m.

Categorized by the users of the network

Public network

This is a large network built at the expense of the Telecommunications Company (state or private) . "public" means that anyone willing to pay a fee under the Telco's rules can use the network. Therefore, the public network can also be called the public network.

Private Network

A private network is a network built by a department to meet the needs of a particular business unit. This network does not provide services to persons outside of the unit. For example, military, railway, banking, power, and other systems have their own private network.

Applications of Computer Network in the Real World

Before going to talk about a brief history of computer networks we will go through a few applications of computer network that has changed our world.

When it comes to computer networks, the first question you have to ask is what they are for, what we can do with them. If you go back more than ten years and ask about the use of computer networks, you might all agree that "resource sharing" is the answer. That was true of computer network applications at the time, and there were no obvious applications other than for resource sharing because there was neither the Internet nor any internal network applications within the LAN. Now, with the improvement and popularization of the computer network system, especially Internet technology, the application of computer network has seen unprecedented prosperity. Computer network Has penetrated into the ordinary people's Daily work, life and leisure, and other aspects.

While there are a lot of computer network applications out there, they fall into two broad categories one is business applications and the other is home / personal applications. Below section shows the detailed description and applications about day to day uses of computer networks.

Commercial Application

Business applications are the most important aspects of computer network applications, and later home / personal applications got developed on the basis of business applications. In the commercial application of computer network, the main network is the corporate Lan, and the internal Lan and Internet of the external users (such as subsidiaries, partners, suppliers, etc.) connected with the Corporate Lan. Business applications include resource sharing, data transmission, collaborative work, remote access and management, e-commerce, etc..

1)Resource sharing

One of the most basic and traditional applications in computer networks is Resource Sharing. The shared resources can be physical devices such as printers, scanners, fax machines, recorders, shared data files, software resources, and so on. The goal is to give everyone access to the devices, programs, files, and data that they allow. One of the simplest examples of resource sharing is when multiple users within a LAN share a printer over the network (some printers now support Internet-shared printing as well) to print there is no need for the company to provide each user with a separate printer, greatly saving equipment investment costs.

More important than physical device sharing in a corporate Lan is the sharing of programs, files, and data resources such as corporate internal public documents, database reports, or software installed by users and the company's database system. The advantage of a Lan is that we no longer have to copy data through removable media (floppy disks, USB sticks, removable hard drives, etc.), as we did in the absence of a computer network. This not only ensures the security of the shared data (because the sharing can also set different access rights for different users) but also greatly improves the efficiency of data sharing usage. Usually, there is a file server in the intranet to store these shared data resources.

There are more examples of resource sharing on the Internet, such as file uploading and downloading, audio and video sharing, file viewing, and viewing, etc..

(2) Network Communication
In the field of network communication, many functions are used in enterprises, such as remote network interconnection, remote

video conference, remote training, remote consultation and so on. The Remote Network Interconnection is currently between the Group Company and the Subsidiary Company or between the company and the partner, the supplier website through the special access way (at present mainly uses the VPN technology) to link each unit's network according to the application demand and the access permission. This can make communication between the network, user access more secure, convenient, but also more effective management of site data and e-commerce data.

Applications such as teleconferencing, remote training, and remote consultation are now common in large corporations and hospitals. On the other hand, the application of this function can save meeting and training cost (because it overcomes the time and space limitation of physical distance), on the other hand, it can make full use of all kinds of expert resources and solve some difficult problems in time.

(3) Data Transmission

Data transmission is most common in computer networks E-MAIL, FTP (File Transfer Protocol) file transfer, TFTP / RCP (simple File Transfer Protocol copy protocol) file upload and download, and so on. For example, we may send files to our friends through WhatsApp or MSN every day, many websites provide the function of downloading resources for users to choose to download the files in their Resource Library Now there are a number of dedicated resources for the upload and download site disk and so on. These processes of uploading and downloading are part of the data transfer application of the computer network.

(4) Working Together

Cooperative work is a typical application of computer network, which means to be in the same or different places through the network Even multiple systems in different countries share the way a particular network communication or network application task works. The most typical example is the load balance of server, switch cluster, many DNS servers in ISP, DC (domain controller) servers and so on can also realize the load balance to provide the corresponding service for the network user.

One of the current applications is the current Wikipedia, where content can be co-edited and refined by globally licensed particIPants. Also, a project can be completed by more than one person in the head office and branch office.

(5) Remote Access and Management

Remote access and management is the way that computer network users access and administrators manage clients and servers. Vpn solutions that support mobile Internet access, for example, allow company employees to connect to the company's network via a VPN at any time, anywhere, to view the files or data they need, and to upload or download the files they need. In addition, using "remote Web desktop" and "remote assistance" functions like those in Windows server systems, employees on business trips can access or even control a host or server on the company's internal network over the Internet. If they have an administrator account, they can also remotely manage and maintain the company's internal servers.

(6) Electronic Commerce

Now almost all the larger units have set up their own websites, one of the purposes is to promote their products to users around the world. In addition, the majority of enterprise users through their own web site to provide customers with online transactions, which is commonly referred to as "e-commerce. ". I'm sure most of you have had the experience of shopping on Amazon, where many businesses have set up shop to sell their wares, ranging from expensive jewelry and household appliances to groceries and books. Others, such as Alibaba, Flipkart and so on (there are so many, so many, so many of them) allow a variety of products to be sold on the site. These e-commerce sites are now commonly referred to as "e-commerce" to distinguish them from brick-and-mortar stores.

Home Applications

In the beginning, the computer network is basically all out of commercial applications, but with the Internet broadband access and the abundance of Internet applications, the computer network began to go into ordinary people's homes. Today, we can access the Internet from our home broadband connection and visit global websites from our home. We can make instant contact with friends and strangers from all over the world through instant messaging software such as Facebook and Twitter; we can also have our own local area networks, or personal websites, which people around the world can visit to learn about the products and services we offer, and the state of our work, school, and life.

Everything that you see in everyday lay comes under Home applications. From Netflix to Spotify to YouTube to WhatsApp. Everything you use in everyday life to communicate, educate yourselves, collaborate with people, plan a travel date or ordering a meal a comes under Home applications. Before moving on further take a paper and note down your best websites and just google how they work for a better understanding of your favorite websites or internet applications.

History of Computer Networking

The purpose of this section is to introduce the history of the development of computer and network. Computers became popular in the 1950s, and their usage patterns have changed a lot since then.

The development of the computer network has gone through several generations of changes. Not only has the connotation of the computer network changed tremendously, but Computer Network Technology and network applications are also no longer the same as a few decades ago, the first and second generation of computer networks can be compared. To understand the whole history of the development of computer network will help us to have a clear understanding of the development of computer network technology and application, and also help us to distinguish which are the mainstream application technologies at present What technologies are out of date that we don't have to learn. Of course, there must be computers before there can be computer networks, just as there must be people before there will be human society. Generally speaking, the development of the computer network can be summarized in the following stages.

(1) First Generation Computer Networks (Terminal-Oriented Computer Networks)

In 1946, the world's first digital computer came out. But there were very few computers and they were very expensive. Since most computers at that time used complex methods, the user computer would first print programs and data into paper tapes or cards, and then send them to the Computing Center for processing. In 1954, a terminal called a Transceiver was introduced, which was used for the first time to transmit data from punched cards over telephone lines to computers in remote computing centers. Since then, teletype has also been connected to a computer as a remote terminal, and users can enter their own programs on a remote teletypewriter and the results calculated by the computer in the computing center can also be sent to a teletypewriter far away and printed out. This simple transmission system was the basic prototype of the computer network. Of course, these are far from us, now we do not have to study these transceiver terminals and their data transmission princIPle.

In order to allow more people to use computers, Batch Processing systems have emerged. Batch processing refers to the way that the user programs and data are loaded into the tape or tape in advance and read by the computer in a certain order so that the programs and data executed by the user can be processed in batch. At that time, this kind of computer was too expensive and bulky to be used in an ordinary office. As a result, they are usually placed in computer centers that specialize in computer management and operations. The user has no choice but to load the program and data onto a cassette or tape in advance and send it to such a center.

At that time, the operation of the computer was very complicated, not all people can easily use. Therefore, in the actual operation of the program will usually be handed over to a special operator to deal with. Sometimes the program takes longer to process, and in the case of a larger number of users, the user program may not run immediately. At this point, the user can only leave the program to the operator and then come back to the computer center to get the results.

The first generation of computer networks was centered around computer hosts (in fact, what we now call "computer servers"), around which one or more terminals were distributed While the task of the computer host is batch processing, the user terminal does not have the ability of data storage and processing. In a sense, this is not a real computer network at all, because the terminal does not have the ability to work independently. So we now say that the birth of computer networks generally does not refer to the first generation of computer networks, but rather to the second generation of computer networks, which is described below. By "terminal", I mean a simple computer made up of a computer's perIPherals, somewhat similar to what we now call "thin clients", consisting only of CRT monitors, keyboards, and no CPU or hard disk So there's no data storage or processing power. The reason why the network is more computer terminal, because the computer is very expensive, in order to save costs, so the client is usually those with no key components of the computer terminal.

A typical application of the first generation of computer networks was the aircraft reservation system Sabre-i, which was developed jointly by American Airlines and IBM in the early 1950s and put into use in the 1960s. It consists of a computer and 2,000 terminals across the United States. The heavy load on the computer in the Computer Center makes the response to the terminal system slow and even brings the phenomenon of a server crash.

The reliability of a single host system is low, once the computer host is paralyzed, the whole computer network system will be paralyzed. Following batch systems, the 1960s saw the emergence of the TSS (Time Sharing System). It refers to a system in which multiple terminals (consisting of input and output devices such as a keyboard, a monitor, and, initially, a typewriter) are connected to the same computer, allowing multiple users to use the same computer at the same time. At that time the computer cost was very expensive, one person a proprietary computer cost for the average person is out of reach. However, the time-sharing system has realized the goal of "one person, one machine", which makes users feel as if "they are using a computer all by themselves". This also reflects the time-sharing system an important feature –Exclusivity.

Since the advent of time-sharing systems, the availability of computers has greatly improved Especially in interactive (interactive) operation (refers to the computer according to the instructions given by the user to complete processing and return the results to the user. This method of operation is extremely common in modern computers, but it was impossible before the advent of time-sharing systems.). Since then, the computer has become more human, gradually close to our lives.

The exclusive nature of the time-sharing system makes it easier than ever to equip a computer environment that users can operate directly. In a time-sharing system, each terminal is connected to a computer using a communication line to form a star-shaped (star-shaped (*) structure with a computer in the center and many terminals around it. It is from this period that the relationship between the network (communication) and the computer.

(2) Second Generation Computer Networks (Packet Switched Computer Networks)

In order to overcome the shortcomings of the first-generation computer network and improve its availability and reliability, experts began to study the method of interconnecting several computers. If there is a problem, solve it. This is the same way that all technologies are now improved. First, the concept of "store-and-forward" (which we will introduce as we learn about switch technology) was introduced in August 1964 by Baran in the Rand Corporation's research paper on distributed communications. Between 1962 and 1965, the Advanced Research Projects Agency (ARPA) in the United States and the National Physics Laboratory (NPL) in the United Kingdom studied the new technology. Later, in 1966, David Davis of the British NPL first introduced the concept of "packet". In December 1969, the world's first computer packet switching system based on packet technology ARPANET was produced. This is widely recognized as the originator of computer networks.

ARPANET was built by the Defense Advanced Research Projects Agency (DARPA) using telephone lines as the backbone of the network. It started with computer s connected to only four nodes -- UCLA, UC Santa Barbara, Stanford, and the University of Utah -- and grew to 15 nodes two years later. By the late 1970s, the network had more than 60 nodes and more than 100 hosts, spanning America and connecting many universities and research institutions in the Eastern and western United States It is also connected to computer networks in Hawaii and across Europe via the communications satellite.

The end-users in the second-generation computer network can share not only the line and equipment resources in the "communication subnet", but also the rich hardware and software resources of the "resource subnet". This "communication subnet" centered computer network became what we now call the second-generation computer network.

(3) Third Generation Computer Networks (Standardized Computer Networks)

By the 1970s, computer performance had soared, size had shrunk, and prices had fallen sharply. So, the computer is no longer limited to the use of research institutions, the general business gradually began to use the computer. That's because there's an increasing boom in the use of computers for day-to-day business. To improve work efficiency, people begin to study the technology of communication between computers.

Before the advent of computer-to-computer communication, it was cumbersome to transfer data from one computer to another.

At that time, data had to be saved to external storage media such as tape and floppy disks (pluggable devices for storing computer information. Originally just disks and floppy disks, now more commonly used electronic storage media such as CD / DVD and USB storage) These media are then sent to the destination computer for data dump. However, with the technology of communication between computers (which are connected by communication lines), it is easy to read data from another computer in real time, thus greatly reducing the time it takes to transmit data

Communication between computers significantly improves the availability of computers. People are no longer limited to using only one computer for processing, but gradually use more than one computer distributed processing, and finally get the results back together. This trend breaks down the situation where a company buys only one computer for business processing and enables the introduction of computers within each company on a departmental basis.

To process data from within the department. After each department has processed its data, it is sent to the computer at headquarters via a communication line and processed by the computer at headquarters to produce the final data results.

Since then, the development of the computer has entered a new historical stage. At this stage, the computer is more focused on meeting the needs of users, a more flexible architecture system, and a more user-friendly operation than before. In the early 1970s, people began to experiment with computer networks based on packet switching technology and began to study the technology of communication between computers of different manufacturers.

The "store-and-forward" mode is adopted in the transmission mode of the second-generation computer network, which greatly improves the utilization ratio of the expensive communication line resources. Because in this "store-and-forward" communication process, communication lines will not be exclusive communication between a certain node but can be shared for multi-channel communication. However, there are still many disadvantages in the second-generation computer network, such as the lack of unified network architecture and protocol standards. Moreover, although the second generation of computer networks has been divided into communication subnetworks and resource subnetworks, the network systems of different companies are only applicable to their own devices and cannot be connected. For example, in 1974, IBM introduced System Network Architecture (SNA) to provide users with a complete set of communications products that can be interconnected, and in 1975, Dec announced its own digital Network Architecture (DNA); In 1976 UNIVAC announced its Distributed Communication Architecture (DCA). These network technology standards are valid only within a single company, comply with certain standards, interconnect network communication products, only apply to equipment produced by the same company.

The network between different companies still can not interconnect. The computer network communication market is such a fragmented situation that users in the direction of investment at a loss, and is not conducive to fair competition between multiple manufacturers.

From the development of the first- and second-generation computer network technologies, we can see that they are driven by enterprises, that is, by companies developing related technologies and products according to their market and user needs Can Be said to be in the "hundred schools of thought" of the Times. Although "a hundred schools of thought" can fully demonstrate the advantages of each company, but after all, "no rules are difficult to square circle. As a result of the competition between these companies, the technologies and products developed by these different companies are not universal. As a result, no one is big or strong, and it is difficult for users to choose the development of the computer network is also very difficult to have substantive progress.

(4) Fourth Generation Computer Networks (International Computer Networks)

By the end of the 1980s, the technology of the local area network (Lan) was mature, and the technology of optical fiber and high-speed Ethernet appeared. With the birth of Osi / RM architecture in the third-generation computer network, it has greatly promoted the development of the Internet represented by the Internet, which is now the fourth generation computer network. The fourth generation of a computer network is defined as "a system that can realize resource sharing and data communication through the network software of communication devices and lines". In fact, the rudiment of the Internet is Darpa's ARPANET, and the protocol standard adopted is TCP / IP Protocol Specification.

The basic history of the Internet is as follows: In 1985, the National Science Foundation established NSFNET, a backbone network for scientific research and education, using the ARPANET protocol; in 1990 NSFnet replaced ARPANET as the backbone of the National Network And out of universities and research institutions into society, from this network of E-mail, file download and information transmission by people's welcome and widespread use; 1992, the establishment of the Internet Society; 1993, the National Center for Supercomputing at the University of Illinois succeeded in developing Mosaic, an online browsing tool that later became Netscape. That same year, Clinton announced the National Information Infrastructure Program Since then, the NSF has competed around the world for leadershIP and supremacy in an information society. At the same time, N SF stopped funding the Internet and fully commercialized it.

In the 1980s, a network capable of interconnecting multiple computers was born. It allows a wide variety of computers to be connected to each other, from large supercomputers or mainframes to small personal computers. A system that processes windows in the. The X Window System, commonly used on UNIX, as well as Microsoft's Windows and Apple's MAC OS X. These systems allow multiple programs to be distributed to run in multiple windows, and switching can be performed in sequence.) The invention of these systems has brought people closer to the web, making users more aware of the Web as a Convenient place. With a windowing system, users can not only execute multiple programs simultaneously but also freely switch jobs between them. For example, while creating a document on a workstation, you can log on to the host to execute other programs, you can download the necessary data from the database server, and you can contact friends via email. With the combination of the window system and network, we can surf the net freely on our own computer and enjoy the rich resources on the net

Into the 1990s, companies and universities focused on information processing had assigned a computer to each employee or researcher, creating a "one person, one machine" environment. However, this environment is not only expensive to build but in the use of the process will also encounter many new problems. That's why the term "downsizing" and "multi-vendor" (here refers to computer hardware or software vendors) was coined. The reason for the two slogans "connection" (a connection between heterogeneous computers) is that a network is built by combining the products of a variety of hardware and software vendors, rather than a single vendor (where both hardware and software are built using the same vendor's products). The goal is to create a lower-cost network environment by connecting computers from different vendors. The communication network technology connecting heterogeneous computers is the Internet technology we see today (in 1990, personal computers connected to local area networks usually used Novell NetWare system. However, when it comes to connecting to all types of computers, such as mainframes, minicomputers, UNIX workstations, and personal computers, TCP / IP is more of a concern

At the same time, ways of spreading information, such as E-mail (E-mail) and the World Wide Web (WWW), have mushroomed, allowing the Internet to spread from large companies to small families Faced with such a trend, manufacturers not only strive to ensure the interconnection of their products but also strive to keep their network technology and internet technology compatibility. These companies are no longer just looking at big businesses, but at every home or Soho (a small office or Home

Office as a place of business), and are rolling out specific web services and products

Now, like the Internet, E-mail, Web, home page and so on has become the most familiar terms. This also suffices to say that the information network, the Internet has penetrated into our lives. The personal computer, which started out as a mostly stand-alone device, is now more widely used for Internet access. And people around the world, no matter how far apart, can communicate and communicate in real time via their personal computers as long as they are connected to the Internet. The popularization and development of the Internet have had a great influence on the field of communication. Many web technologies with different paths are also moving closer to the Internet. For example, used to be used as a communication base.

By the Internet Protocol Network, which itself is the product of Internet technology. Through the IP network, people can not only realize. Now telephone communications, television broadcast, but also to achieve communication between computers, the establishment of the Internet. Also, devices that connect to the Internet. The Internet has allowed people from all over the world to connect freely across borders via computers. The Internet allows people to search for information, communicate, share information, view news reports, and control devices remotely. However, it's so convenient. The original purpose of a computer network was to connect individual computers to form a more powerful computing environment. In short, to increase productivity. From the age of batch processing to the age of computer networks, there is no doubt that this is the case. Now, however, there seems to be a subtle shift

One of the primary purposes of modern computer networks can be said to be to connect people. People around the world can connect, communicate and exchange ideas via the Internet. This, however, was not possible in the early days of computer networks. This human-to-human computer network has gradually brought about great changes in people's daily life, school education, Scientific Research, and company development. The vast majority of people know the Internet from the first contact with the application of the Internet. Now children can play games online, watch online videos, or chat with friends on Whatsapp. More adults are regularly searching and accessing information on the Internet. Now people often use the Internet to communicate with each other by e-mail (including the transmission of a variety of photos and video files), which makes the traditional postal mail business volume greatly reduced. Buying all kinds of goods on the internet is both convenient and economical, changing the way you have to shop. The purchase of air or train tickets on the Internet can save a lot of queuing time and greatly facilitate passengers. On the financial front, the use of the Internet for transactions such as money transfers or stock trading can save a lot of time.

(5) Next Generation Computer Network

Some people will ask, in what era are we now on the computer? It can be said that we are now in a transitional period between the fourth and fifth generations. But in the end, no one can say for sure what the next generation network will look like, at least not by a long shot. Generally speaking, it is generally believed that the next generation computer network (NGN, that is to say, the Fifth Generation Computer Network) is the convergence of Internet, Mobile Communication Network, fixed telephone communication network, IP network, an optical network. It is an integrated and open network framework that can provide various services including voice, data, and multimedia, and it is a service driven, service and call control separate, call and carry separate network; Is a unified protocol-based, packet-based network. In terms of function, Ngn is divided into four layers, namely access and transmission layer, media layer, control layer, and network service layer. We can see some of the main features of the next-generation computer network, including The current is the "three networks" (computer network, telecommunications network, television network) integration, the Internet of things, virtualization, cloud computing, HTML5, and other new revolutionary technologies.

Among these new technologies, "cloud computing" and "Internet of things" may be the two most important technologies that will revolutionize the current landscape and applications of computer networks in the future. "Cloud Computing" is really similar to the IBM mainframe, is a centralized service, centralized management platform. Is for cloud computing operators to provide enterprise customers with a number of software, hardware platforms and a variety of required services and management, enterprise customers can enjoy the services and platforms they buy simply by connecting to the cloud computing platform of the operator located on the Internet through a relatively simple cloud computing client The investment of enterprise clients in computer network software and hardware platform (such as various server systems, enterprise switches, routers, firewalls, etc.) is greatly saved.

The Internet of things (IOT) is a new technology that continues to expand computer networks. It is simply the Internet of things. It uses radio frequency identification (RFID) technology, as well as infrared sensors, Global Positioning System, laser scanners and other information sensing devices, according to agreed protocols Connecting items (such as electric lights, electrical appliances, monitoring facilities, etc.) that are not currently connected to the computer network to the Internet for information exchange and communication between items, to achieve the intelligent identification, positioning, tracking, monitoring and management of items. Through the "Internet of things" we will be able to control the work at home lights, electrical equipment switches, monitoring home security monitoring facilities, truly ubiquitous internet applications.

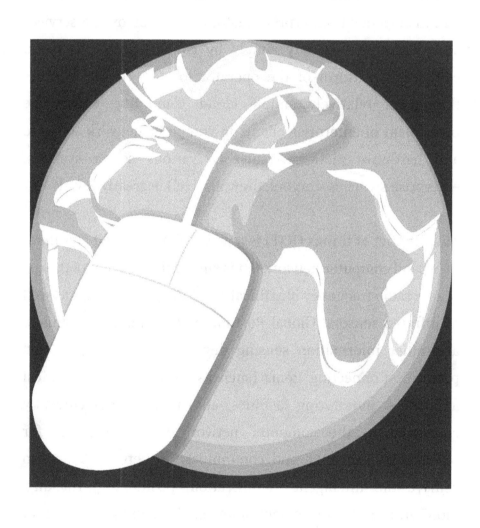

Chapter 2: Computer Networking Basics

Before discussing in detail about computer networks, we will first discuss Internet, the biggest network in the detail and few protocols in which it communicates with the end user for a better understanding of the Network architecture.

Why the Internet Has Become a Sensation?
The reason why the Internet can provide many services to users is that the Internet has two important basic characteristics, namely connectivity, and sharing.

Connectivity is when the Internet allows users to connect to each other, no matter how far apart they are (thousands of kilometers, for example) All kinds of information (data, as well as audio and video) can be exchanged very easily, very cheaply (and in many cases, free of charge), as if these user terminals were all connected directly to each other. This is quite different from using a traditional telecommunications network.

The Internet has become the largest computer network in the world, let's start with an overview of the Internet, including the main components of the Internet, so that we can have a preliminary understanding of the computer network.
The network connects many computers together, while the Internet connects many networks through routers. A computer

connected to a network is often called a mainframe. The Internet has become the world's largest and fastest growing computer network, and no one can say exactly how big it is. The rapid development of the Internet began in the 1990s. The World Wide Web (WWW) developed by CERN, the European Organization for Nuclear Research, is widely used on the Internet, greatly facilitating the use of the Internet by non-network Professionals Has Been The main driver of this exponential growth of the Internet. The number of sites on the World Wide Web has also increased dramatically. Accurate traffic on the Internet is difficult to estimate, but the literature suggests that data traffic on the Internet is increasing by about 10 percent per month.

The part on the edge of the Internet is all the hosts that are connected to the Internet. These hosts are also called end systems, and "end" means "end" (the end of the Internet). End Systems can vary widely in function. A small end system can be an ordinary personal computer (including a laptop or tablet) and a smartphone with Internet access Even a small Webcam (which can monitor local weather or traffic and post it on the Internet in real time), and a large end-system can be a very expensive mainframe computer. The owner of an end system can be an individual, a unit (such as a school, an enterprise, a government agency, etc.), or an ISP (that is, an ISP can own some end systems as well as provide services to the end system). The edge uses the services provided by the core to enable multiple hosts to communicate with each other and exchange or share information.

Communication in the Internet

We need to define the following concepts. When we say "host a communicates with host B, " we actually mean that "a program running on host a communicates with another program running on host B. ". Since "process" is "running program", this means that "a process on host a communicates with another process on host B. ". This more rigorous approach is often referred to simply as "computer-to-computer communication. ". Communication between end systems at the edge of the network can usually be divided into two categories: client-server mode (C / s mode) and peer-to-peer mode (P2P mode). These two approaches are described below.

Client-Server Approach

This is the most common and traditional approach to the Internet. We use the client-server mode (sometimes written as client/server mode) when we go online to send e-mails or look up information on the web site. When we make a call, the ringing of the telephone alerts the called user that there is now a call. The object of computer communication is the application process in the application layer. Obviously, the application process cannot be notified by ringing. However, the client-server approach enables the two application processes to communicate.

Both client and server are the two application processes involved in communication. The client-server approach describes the relationship between the services and the serviced processes. Host A runs the client program and host B runs the server program. In this case, a is the client and B is the server. Client A makes a service request to server B, and Server B serves client A.

The main features here are:

The client is the service requester and the server is the service provider.

Both the service requester and the service provider use the services provided by the core part of the network. In practice, client and server programs typically also have some of the following main features.

Client Program:

(1) Running after being invoked by the user, initiating communication (requesting service) to the remote server during communication. Therefore, the client must know the address of the server program.

(2) no special hardware or complex operating system is required.

Server application:

(1) Is a program designed to provide a service that can handle requests from multiple remote or local customers simultaneously.

(2) the system is called automatically after starting up and is running continuously, passively waiting for and receiving communication requests from customers from all over the world. Therefore, the server program does not need to know the address of the client program.

(3) Strong hardware and advanced operating system support are generally required.

By the way, both the client and the server referred to above refer to computer processes (software). The person using the computer is the "user" of the computer, not the "client". But in many foreign pieces of literature, the machine that runs the client program is often called client (in this case client can also be translated as "client"), and the machine that runs the server program is called server. So, we should judge whether the client or server refers to software or hardware according to the context. In this book, we also use "client" (or "client") or "Server" (or server) to refer to a "machine that runs a client program" or "machine that runs a server program" when referring to a machine.

Peer to Peer Connections

Peer-to-peer, P2P. The number 2 is used here because the English word 2 is two, which is pronounced the same as to, so the English word to is often abbreviated to the number 2) refers to two hosts communicating without distinguishing between the service requester and the service provider. As long as both hosts are running peer-to-peer (P2P) software, they can communicate on an equal, peer-to-peer basis. At this point, each party can download a shared document that the other party has stored on its hard drive. So, this way of working is also called P2P. The hosts C, D, E, and fall run P2P software, so the hosts can communicate peer-to-peer (such as C and D, E and F, and C and F). In fact, peer-to-peer connectivity is still essentially a client-server approach, except that each host in a peer-to-peer connection is both a client and a server. For example, host C, when c requests the services of D, C is the client and D is the server. But if C serves F at the same time, c serves as a server.

Peer-to-peer connections work in a way that allows a large number of peer users, such as one million, to work at the same time. BitTorrent is the best example for a peer to peer connections.

From typing a URL into a browser to displaying the contents of a web page on a screen, in a matter of seconds, many pieces of hardware and software work together in their respective roles. Each of the individual links is not complicated, as long as you read carefully will be able to understand. However, there is so much hardware and software involved in the journey that if you focus on each individual point from a micro perspective, you may lose sight of the whole and lose your way. So before we set out to explore, let's take a brief look at this journey. The following introduction also contains a road map for a journey of discovery, in case you get lost on the way.

The Complete Picture of the Web

Let's first take a look at the full picture of how a browser accesses a Web server. The process of accessing a Web server and displaying a Web page involves a series of interactions between the Browser and the Web server, primarily the following.

(1) Browser: "Please give me the web page data. "
(2) Web
(2) Web Server: "Ok will do it"

After this series of interactions is complete, the browser displays the data it receives from the Web server on the screen. While the process of displaying a web page is complex, the interaction between the browser and the server over the network is surprisingly simple. When we shop in an online mall, we type in the name of the product and the address of the goods we want to receive and send it to a Web server.

(1) Browser: "please process these order data. "

(2) Web

(2) Web Server: "okay, Order Data received.

While the actual processing of an order with the sales system after the Web server receives the order data is complex, the interaction between the Browser and the Web server is simple, as summarized below.

(1) the browser sends a request to the Web server.

(2) Web

(3) The Web server sends a response to the browser based on the request.

So at this level, where Web applications like browsers and Web servers interact, it should be relatively easy to understand how it works. The interaction at this level is very similar to the dialogue between humans and is easier to understand from this point 1.

To enable interaction between applications, we need a mechanism to pass requests and responses between the Browser and the Web server. The network is composed of many computers and other devices connected to each other, so in the process of communication, we need to determine the correct communication object and send the request and response to them. Requests and responses can be lost or corrupted during delivery, so these situations must also be considered. So we need a mechanism to send requests and responses to each other without fail, no matter what the situation. Since the request and response are both 0 and 1 pieces of digital information, it can be said that we need a mechanism to carry the digital information to the designated destination.

This mechanism is implemented by the network control software in the operating system, as well as the division of labor between switches, routers and other devices. Its basic idea is to divide the digital information into small pieces It is then shIPped in containers called "packs". The word "Bag" is a word that you may often come across when using a mobile phone, but here it is similar to the concept used in postal and courier services.

You can think of a package as a letter or package, and a switch or router as a sorting area for a post office or a delivery company. The header of the packet contains the destination information, which can be sorted according to the relay of many switches and routers, and then carried to the destination step by step. Whether it's a home and corporate LAN, or the Internet out there, they're just different in size, and the underlying mechanisms are the same.

Together with Web applications such as browsers and Web servers, these two parts of the Web make up the Web. That is to say, these two parts are put together, the whole picture of the network.

We'll start by exploring how the browser works. You can think of our exploration as starting with typing a URL into your browser. Of course, the browser is not personally responsible for the transfer of data. The mechanism that carries the digital information is responsible for sending the message, so the browser delegates the data to it. Specifically, the network control software in the operating system is delegated to send messages to the server.

One of the first to appear is the protocol stack (network control software called Protocol Stack). The software packages the messages it receives from the browser and adds control information such as the destination address. To use the post office analogy is to put the letter in an envelope and write the addressee's address on the envelope.

The software also has other functions, such as resending packets in the event of a communication error or adjusting the rate at which data is sent, perhaps we can think of it as a little secretary who helps us send letters.

Next, the stack hands the packet to the network card (the hardware responsible for Ethernet or wireless network communications). The Network Card then converts the packet into an electrical signal and sends it out over the wire. In this way, the packet enters the network.

What comes next will vary according to the form of Internet access. A client computer can access the Internet either through a home or corporate Lan or directly on its own. Unfortunately, our exploration does not cover all of these possibilities, so we have to assume, for example, that the client computer is connected to a home or Corporate Lan Then through ADSL and fiber to the home (FTTH) and other broadband lines to access the Internet.

In such a scenario, packets sent by a network card pass through a switch or other device to a router used to access the Internet. Behind the router is the Internet, and the network operator is responsible for delivering the package to the destination, just as the postman is responsible for delivering the letter to the recIPient after we drop it into the mailbox.

The data then travels from the router used to access the Internet to the inside of the Internet. The gateway to the Internet is called the access network. In general, we can use telephone lines, Isdn, Adsl, cable television, light, private lines, and other communication lines to access the Internet, these communication lines collectively known as an access network. An access network connects to a contracted network operator and to a device called a Point of Presence (PoP).

The entity of the access point is a router designed for the operator, which we can think of as the nearest post office to your home. Letters collected from various mailboxes are sorted at post offices and then sent around the country or even around the world, as is the case with the Internet, where packets are first sent through an access network to an access point and then sent from here to the rest of the country and the world. Behind the access point is the backbone of the Internet.

There are many operators and a large number of routers in the backbone network. These routers are connected to each other to form a huge network, and our network packet is passed through the relay of several routers Is eventually sent to the target Web server. The details are explained in the main text, but the basic principle is the same as that of home and corporate routers. That is to say, whether on the Internet or in the home, Corporate Lan, packets are transmitted in the same way, which is a major feature of the Internet.

However, the router used by the operators is different from the small router we use at home. It is a high-speed large router that can connect dozens of network lines. In the backbone of the Internet, there are a large number of these routers, they are connected to each other in a complex way, and network packets are passing through these routers.

In addition, routers differ not only in size but also in the way they connect to each other. Ethernet cables are commonly used in home and corporate LANs, while the Internet uses older telephony and the latest optical communication technologies to transmit network packets in addition to Ethernet connections. The technology used in this section is the most popular part of today's network, can be said to be the crystallization of the most sophisticated technology.

After passing through the backbone network, the network packet finally arrives in the local Area Network where the Web server is located.

Next, it encounters a firewall, which checks the incoming packets. Think of the firewall as the security guard at the door, who checks all the bags that come in to see if any of the dangerous bags are in there. After the check, the network packet may then encounter the cache server. A portion of the web page data is reusable, and this reusable data is stored in the cache server. If the page data you want to access happens to be found in the cache server, you can read the data directly from the cache server without bothering the Web server. In addition, in large Web sites, there may be load balancers that distribute messages across multiple Web servers, and there may be services that distribute content through caching servers distributed across the Internet. After these mechanisms, the network packets arrive at the Web server.

When the network packet arrives at the Web Server, the data is unpacked and restored to the original request message, which is then handed over to the Web server program. Like the client, this is done by the protocol stack (network control software) in the operating system. Next, the Web server program analyzes the meaning of the request message, loads the data into the response message as instructed, and then sends it back to the client. The process of returning the response message to the client is exactly the opposite of what we described earlier.

When the response reaches the client, the browser reads the data from the web page and displays it on the screen. At this point, a series of operations to access the Web server are complete, and our journey of discovery has come to an end

How the Internet is Connected?

This Network is the Access Network AN (Access Network), which is also known as the local Access Network, or resident Access Network. This is a special kind of computer network. As we explained above, a user must be able to access the Internet through an ISP. Since there are many technologies available for accessing the Internet from a user's home, there are situations where multiple access network technologies can be used to connect to the Internet. The access network itself is neither the core nor the periphery of the Internet. An access network is a network between a client system and the first router (also known as an edge router) on the Internet. From the scope of coverage, many access networks also belong to local area networks. From the point of view of the role, the access network is only to allow users to connect with the Internet "bridge" role. In the early days of the Internet, users used telephone lines to dial into the Internet at very low rates (from a few thousand to a few tens of thousands of bits per second), so the term access network was not used.

Basic Components of Computer Network

No matter which definition can be seen above, the computer network is a complete system composed of some hardware equipment and corresponding software system. The basic components of a computer network include a computer (or a computer terminal with only basic computer functions), network connections and communication equipment, transmission media, and network communication software (including network communication protocols).

These basic computer network components are divided into hardware systems and software systems.

Computer Network Hardware System

Computer Network hardware system refers to the visible physical facilities in the computer network, including all kinds of computer equipment, transmission media, network equipment, these three major parts.

1. Computer Equipment

The purpose of building a computer network is to provide a platform for network communication among users of various computer equipment, such as user access, data transmission, file sharing, remote control and so on. A computer device is a variety of computers (such as pcs, computer servers, computer terminals, laptop computers, IPad and the like) that are controlled and used by network users. The main applications of the network are performed on these computer devices. In fact, now the computer network and the telecommunication network are somewhat overlapped. Many telecommunication terminals can also be connected to the computer network, such as the smartphones we use now Can carry on the data transmission between the USB interface and the computer, even carries on the remote communication.

Note that in the traditional definition of a computer network, a computer network requires at least one fully functional physical computer (others can be terminals). With the rise of Network virtualization technology, the current computer network can be a virtual machine (such as VPC, VMWare, etc.) in a physical computer simulation of a number of independent computer systems, forming a virtual computer network This network can also perform functions that can only be performed in many physical computer networks.

2. Network Equipment

In a computer network system, network equIPment usually refers to equIPment other than computer equIPment Such as network card, bridge, gateway, Modem, switch, router, hardware firewall, hardware IDS (intrusion detection system), hardware

IPS (intrusion prevention system) , broadband access server (Bras) , UPS (uninterruptible power supply) , etc. Wlan Network Card, WLAN AP, WLAN Router, WLAN switch, etc.

Network equipment is used to construct the network topology in the "communication subnet", and the communication lines (that is, "transmission medium") together to form the framework of the whole computer network. Of course, the simplest network, in fact, does not need any network equipment, that is, two terminal computers with serial/parallel port cable directly connected to the peer-to-peer network. But this network is not really a computer network, for now, such a computer network does not have much practical significance.

3. Transmission Medium

The transmission medium is simply the network line, is the network communication "road". Without these transmission media, the network communication signal will not know where to transmit, also cannot transmit, just like there is no road ahead, we cannot move forward. Of course, the transmission medium can be physically tangible, such as coaxial cable (which is also used in cable television), twisted pair, optical cable (also known as an optical fiber), etc, or invisible For example, the transmission medium used in various wireless networks is, in fact, electromagnetic waves. Wireless Computer Network (WCN) is to realize the connection of each node in WCN by the electromagnetic wave. Of course, in the coaxial cable, twisted pair, optical cable, and these transmission media.

4. Computer Network Software System

Computer Network communication in addition to the aforementioned various computer hardware systems, but also some computer network communication and application software. These computer network communication and application software refer to the computer program installed in the terminal computer for computer network communication or application. First of all, there is a network application platform, such as computers and servers installed, with the computer network communication functions of the operating system. Operating Systems for computer network communications are also installed on devices such as switches, routers, and firewalls. For example, Windows, Linux, UNIX, CatOS for Cisco Switch/router/ Firewall, IOS for IOS, and Comware for H3C switch/router/ firewall.

In addition to the operating system, the network communication protocols, such as TCP / IP Protocol Cluster, Ieee 802 protocol cluster, PPP, PPPoE, IPX / SPX, and VLAN, STP, RIP, OSPF, BGP, etc. Finally, it is necessary to carry out a variety of specific network applications tool software, such as our common Qq, MSN instant messaging software, Outlook, Firefox, Sendmail and other email software, for dial-up PPP, PPPoE protocol IPSEC, PPTP, L2TP and so on for VPN communication.

How the Internet is given to people?

Internet Communications

Let's take a closer look at how the actual network is constructed. People generally use Internet access services when they connect to the Internet at home or at work. With the Internet, the traffic that converges to the Wireless Lan router and the nearest switch is again connected to the "access layer" mentioned earlier (sometimes directly to the "Edge Network" if the company is large, the network is large, or there is a lot of external access). It is even possible to communicate with the target address through an "edge network" or "backbone".

Mobile Communications

As soon as the phone is turned on, it will automatically communicate wirelessly with the nearest base station. The base station is equipped with a special cell phone base antenna, and the base itself is the "access layer" of the network. When a cell phone terminal sends a signal to another terminal, the request goes all the way to the base station that registers the phone number on the other end. If the other party answers the call, a communication connection is established between the two phones. The communications requests collected by the base station are collected in the Control Center ("Edge Network"), which is then connected to the backbone of the Interconnection Control Center. This mobile network is structured much like an Internet access service.

LTE and Voice Call

His limited data communications. And LTE is regarded as the transition technology from 3G to 4G, which is a kind of mobile communication standard made by 3GPP (the organization that makes the 3rd Generation Mobile Communication Standard made up of standardization bodies in different countries). Depending on the situation, it can achieve up to 300 Mbps down and 75 MBPS UP wireless communications.

In the LTE standard, the use of TCP / IP over the entire network is necessary because the voice is also transmitted as an IP packet. (today, voice communications are also largely digital, using TCP / IP Technology.). However, in reality, it is often impossible to replace all the hardware devices in the network all at once. In this case, the techniques of CSFB (CSFB) can be used. The technology allows voice calls to be transmitted only over cellular networks. Keeps it in line with the original sound process.

Chapter 3: Networking in Detail

The original purpose of a computer network was to connect individual computers to form a more powerful computing environment. In short, to increase productivity. From the age of batch processing to the age of computer networks, there is no doubt that this is the case that computer networks are intended to. Now, however, there seems to be a subtle shift in technology.

One of the primary purposes of modern computer networks can be said to be to connect people. People around the world can connect, communicate and exchange ideas via the Internet. This, however, was not possible in the early days of computer networks. This human-to-human computer network has gradually brought about great changes in people's daily life, school education, Scientific Research, and company development.

This chapter describes in much detail about computer networking architecture in such a way that it can enrich your minds and helps you understand the complex process that goes on in computer networking. A few examples and situations will be used for your better understanding of the topic.

Protocol

In the field of computer network and information communication, people often refer to the word "protocol". The representative protocols in common use on the internet are IP, TCP, HTTP and so on. The protocols commonly used in Lan (local area network) are IPX / SPX (NetWare system protocol developed by Novell) and so on.

Why protocols are needed?

Typically, we send an E-mail, visit a home page to get information and are unaware of the protocol that goes on in the background, which is only possible if we reconfigure the computer's network connection and modify network settings. So as long as the network is set up and connected successfully, people often forget about protocols and things. As long as the application knows how to leverage the protocols, it should be enough to allow people to use the network connection they have built. It is not uncommon for a person to be unable to access the Internet because they do not understand certain protocols. However, in the process of communication through the network, the protocol plays a vital role and as you are keen on knowing about protocols can give you a good overview of the topic.

In a word, the protocol is a kind of "agreement" that the client computer and the server computer realize the communication through the network. This "convention" allows computers that are made up of different devices from different vendors, different

CPUs, and different operating systems to communicate with each other as long as they follow the same protocol. On the other hand, if different protocols are used, communication cannot be achieved. It's like two people speaking in different languages who can't understand each other. There are many types of protocols, each of which clearly defines its code of conduct. Two computers must be able to support the same protocol, and follow the same protocol for processing, so as to achieve mutual communication. Before starting to dwell on the topic of protocols further let us discuss two very basic things that you need to know for better understanding. They are the central processing unit and operating system.

CPU

CPU (Central Processing Unit). It's like the "heart" of a computer, every program Is actually scheduled and executed by it. The performance of the CPU also determines the processing performance of a computer to a great extent. So people often say that the history of the computer is actually the history of the CPU. At present, people often use CPU Intel Core, Intel Atom, ARM CORTEX, and other products.

Operating System

Os (Operating System) Operating System, is a kind of basic software. It integrates the CPU management, memory management, computer perIPherals management, and program management and other important functions. The treatment of

TCP or IP protocols described here, in many cases is already embedded in specific operating systems. Today's operating systems commonly used in personal computers are UNIX, Windows, Mac OS x, Linux, and so on.

The instructions that can be run in a computer vary from one CPU to another and from one operating system to another. Therefore, programs designed for certain CPUs or operating systems may not run directly if they are copied directly to computers with other types of CPUs or operating systems. The data stored in a computer also varies from CPU to the operating system. Therefore, if the CPU and the operating system between different computers to achieve communication, IT needs a party to support the protocol, and follow this protocol for data reading. This is the reason why you can't run an android app in an iPhone.

In addition, a CPU can usually only run one program at a time. In order to make multiple programs run at the same time, the operating system adopts the CPU time slice rotation mechanism to switch between multiple programs and schedule reasonably. This approach is called multitasking.

So What Is An Agreement In Protocol?
Agreements are like conversations between people. Here's a simple example. There's three of them. Sam, Tom, and Jerry. Sam can only speak Chinese, Tom can only speak English, and Jerry can speak both Chinese and English. Now Sam and Tom

need to talk. How should they communicate with each other? What if Tom and Jerry need to talk?

If we: Treat Chinese and English as "agreements. " Use Chat communication"

And Treat what you say as "data. "

I am afraid that Sam and Tom cannot communicate with each other for as long as they speak in one language. Because of the difference in the agreement (language) used in their conversation, neither party is able to transmit the data (what is said) to the other party. (a simultaneous interpreter between the two can facilitate communication, as the gateway does in a network environment.)

Next, we analyze the conversation between Sam and Jerry. By using this "agreement" in Chinese, two people can understand what the other person is trying to say. That is to say, Sam and Jerry use the same protocol in order to communicate smoothly so that they can transmit the desired data (what they want to say to each other).

In this sense, agreements are like the language of ordinary speech. Although language is a human property, when computers communicate with each other over the Internet, it can also be argued that communication is based on something akin to human "language" (similarly, some of the actions we take for granted in our daily lives are in many cases consistent with the concept of "agreement").

Protocols in Computers

Human beings have the ability to master knowledge, and they also have a certain ability to apply and understand knowledge. So in a way, human communication isn't limited by too many rules. Even if there are any rules and the like, people can adapt to the rules naturally through their ability to adapt. However, all of this in computer communication, obviously impossible to achieve. Because the level of computer intelligence has not reached the level of human beings. In fact, everything from the physical connection level of a computer to the software level of an application must be followed exactly.

True communication can only be achieved by a prior agreement. In addition, each computer must be equipped with programs that perform the most basic functions of communication. If you replace Sam, Tom, and Jerry in the previous example with a computer, it's easy to understand why you need to clearly define protocols, and why you should follow established protocols to design software and build computer hardware.

People usually do not need special attention when speaking to be able to naturally enunciate, pronunciation. And on many occasions, human beings can adjust their expressions and what they want to convey according to each other's semantics, voice or expression, so as to avoid misunderstanding. Sometimes even in the course of the conversation if accidentally miss a few words, also from the context and context of the conversation to guess the general meaning of the other party to express, not to affect their understanding. But computers can't do that. Therefore, in the design of computer programs and hardware, we should take full account of the communication process may encounter a variety of exceptions and exception handling. When a problem is actually encountered, the computers communicating with each other must also have the appropriate equipment and programs to deal with the exception.

In computer communication, it is important to reach a detailed agreement in advance and follow it. This kind of agreement is actually "agreement" in the protocol.

Packet Switching Protocol

Packet switching is a method of splitting large data into smaller units called packets for transmission. The bag in question is the same as the one we usually see in the post office. Packet switching is the act of breaking up big data into such packets and handing them off to each other.

When people mail a package, they usually fill out a mailing form, attach it to the package and hand it to the post office. The mailing list usually has the full address of the sender and recIPient. Similarly, computer communications will attach the source host address and the destination host address to each packet sent to the communication line. The sender address, the receiver address, and the part of the packet number written are called the "packet header ".

When a larger piece of data is divided into groups, it is necessary to write the ordinal number of the group into the package in order to identify which part of the original data is. Based on this sequence number, the receiver reassembles each packet into the original data.

In a communication protocol, it is common to specify what information should be written at the beginning of the message and how it should be handled. Each computer that communicates with each other constructs the first part of the message and reads the first part of the content according to the protocol. In order for the two parties to communicate correctly, it is necessary for the sender and the receiver of the packet to keep consistent definition and interpretation of the first part and content of the packet.

So, who regulates the communication protocol? In order to enable computers from different manufacturers to communicate with each other, there is an organization that sets standards for communication protocols and defines international standards. In the next section, we will elaborate on the protocol's standardization process.

The Birth and Standardization of Computer Communications

At the beginning of computer communication, systematization and standardization did not get enough attention. Each computer manufacturer produces its own network products to enable computer communications. No strong sense of systematization, layering, etc. In 1974, IBM released the SNA, which exposed the company's computer communications technology as a systematic network architecture. Since then, computer manufacturers have also released their own network architecture, triggering the systematization of many protocols. However, the various network architectures and protocols of various manufacturers are not compatible with each other. Even if two heterogeneous computers are connected on the physical level, normal communication cannot be realized because of the different network architecture and the different protocols.

This is extremely inconvenient for the user. Because this means that the computer network products of which vendor was used in the first place can only be used from the same vendor all the time. If the relevant vendor goes bankrupt or the product exceeds its service life, the entire network equipment must be replaced. In addition, it is not uncommon for different departments to be unable to communicate even when they are physically connected to each other because the network products used are not the same. The lack of flexibility and extensibility made it difficult for users to use computer communication freely.

With the increasing importance of computers, many companies have come to realize the importance of compatibility. People began to work on technologies that would allow heterogeneous models produced by different manufacturers to communicate with each other. This promotes the openness and versatility of the web.

In order to solve these problems, ISO (International Organization for Standards) has established an International standard, Osi (Open Systems Interconnection reference model), and standardized the communication system. Currently, OSI protocols are not commonly used, but the OSI reference model, which was the guideline of Osi Protocol design, is often used in the development of network protocols.

The standardization of the protocol also enables all devices that follow the standard protocol to no longer be unable to communicate due to differences in computer hardware or operating systems. Therefore, the standardization of protocols has also promoted the popularization of computer networks.

In the real world, there are many good technologies that are not widely available because their development companies do not publish the appropriate development specifications. If companies can make their development specifications public, and more of their peers can use them in time and become industry standards, then there will be more and better products that can survive and be used by us.

OSI reference model

Before ISO standardized Osi, the related problems of network architecture were fully discussed, and the OSI reference model was proposed as a communication protocol design index. This model divides the necessary functions of the communication protocol into 7 layers. Through these layers, the more complex network protocols are simplified. In this model, each layer receives a specific service provided by its lower layer and is responsible for providing a specific service to its upper layer. The conventions that govern the interaction between upper and lower layers are called "interfaces. ". The conventions that govern interactions between layers are called protocols.

Protocol layering is like modular development in computer software. The recommendations of the OSI reference model are ideal. It wants to implement all the modules from the first layer to the seventh layer and combine them to achieve network communication. Layering allows each layer to be used independently, so that even if some of the layering changes in the system, it does not affect the whole system. Therefore, it is possible to construct a system that is both extensible and flexible. In addition, by layering the communication functions can be subdivided, making it easier to implement separate protocols for each layering and to define the specific responsibilities and obligations of each layering. These are all advantages of layering. The downside of layering may be over modularity, making processing more burdensome, and having to implement similar processing logic for each module.

Understanding Layering Through a Simple Example

First, take telephone chat as an example. two people, Adam and Eve, are talking on the telephone (communication device) in English (language protocol). On the surface, Adam and Eve are having a direct conversation in English, but in reality, Adam and Eve are both listening to the voice on the receiver of the telephone, both speaking into the microphone. Imagine what a person who has never seen a telephone would think if they saw this? I'm afraid he must think Adam and Eve are talking on the telephone in networking perspective.

The language protocol they use in an audio input to the microphone is translated into radio signals at the communications device level. Sent to each other's phones, and then converted to audio output by the communications equipment layer, passed to each other. Thus, Adam and Eve actually have a conversation using an interface between the telephone and the voice converted by audio.

People often think that when they pick up the phone to talk to someone, it's as if they're talking to them directly, but if you look closely, it's really the phone that's mediating the whole process, and there's no denying that. What if the electronic signals from Adam's phone were not converted into sounds of the same frequency as those from Eve's? This is similar to the difference in protocol between Adam's phone and Eve's phone. Eve May hear the voice and feel that he is not talking to Adam, but to someone else. If the frequencies are far apart, Eve is more likely to think he is not hearing English.

So what if we change the communication device layer by assuming that the language layer is the same. For example, change the telephone to a radio. If the communication equIPment layer uses the radio, they must learn to use the radio method. Since the language layer is still using the English protocol, users can talk just as normally as they used to when they were on the phone.

So, what if the communication device layer uses a telephone and the language layer changes to English? It is clear that the telephone itself will not be limited by the user's language. Therefore, this situation and the use of English calls exactly the same, still can be achieved call.

The previous example simply divides the protocol into two layers. However, the actual packet communication protocols can be quite complex. The OSI reference model organizes such a complex protocol into seven easy-to-understand layers.

OSI Reference Model

The OSI reference model does a good job of summarizing the necessary functions for communication. Network engineers also often prototype the layers of the OSI reference model when discussing protocol-related issues. For beginners in computer networks, learning the OSI reference model can be the first step to success.

The OSI reference model is, after all, a "model, " a rough set of definitions of what each layer does, without a detailed definition of the protocol and interface. It serves only as a guide to learning and designing protocols. Therefore, if you want to know more details about the agreement, it is necessary to refer to the specific specifications of each agreement itself.

Many communication protocols correspond to one of the seven layers of the OSI reference model. From this, we can get a general idea of the position and function of the protocol in the whole communication function. While it takes a careful reading of the specification to understand the protocol, its general purpose can be found at the corresponding OSI model layer. This is why the OSI model is the first to be studied before learning about each protocol.

The OSI (Reference Model) divides communication functions into seven layers, called the OSI reference model. The OSI Protocol, based on the OSI Reference Model, defines the protocol and interface-related standards for each layer. Products that follow the OSI Protocol are called Osi products, and the communications they follow are called Osi Communications. Do not confuse "Osi reference model" with "OSI protocol" because of their different meanings.

The OSI layers are presentation layer, application layer, session layer, transport layer, Network layer, Data link layer, and physical layer. Below we explain all these layers briefly.

Application layer

Provides services to the application and specifies the communication-related details in the application. Including file transfer, email, remote login (virtual terminal) and other protocols.

Presentation Layer

Convert the information processed by the application into a format suitable for network transmission, or convert the data from the next layer into a format that the upper layer can handle. Therefore, it is mainly responsible for data format conversion. Specifically, the device will be inherent in the data format into the network standard transmission format. Different devices may interpret the same bitstream differently. Therefore, making them consistent is the main function of this layer.

Session Layer

Responsible for establishing and disconnecting communication links (logical path of data flow) and data transfer related tubes such as data partitioning manager.

Transport Layer

It acts as a reliable transmitter. Processing is done only on both sides of the communication, not only on the router.

Network Layer

Transfer data to the destination address. The destination address can be a single address that is connected to multiple networks via a router. Therefore, this layer is mainly responsible for addressing and routing.

Data Link Layer

Responsible for the physical level of interconnection, communication between the nodes. For example, communication between two nodes connected to one Ethernet network. The 0,1 sequence is divided into meaningful data frames and transmitted to the opposite end (generation and reception of data frames).

Physical Layer

Responsible for the 0,1-bit current (0,1 sequence) and voltage levels, light flash between the exchange.

After the brief explanation of the reference model, you may be quite confused with new terms. So Here we explain with a small example to make you understand the communication between the OSI layers in detail.

How Do You Modularize Communications in the 7-layer OSI MODEL?

The sender transmits data sequentially from Layer 7, layer 6 to Layer 1, while the receiver transmits data from Layer 1, layer 2 to layer 7 down to each upper layer. At each layer, the data from the previous layer can be processed with the "first" information necessary for the current hierarchical protocol. Then the receiving end of the data received from the "first" and "content" of the separation, and then forward to the next layer, and finally the sending end of the data back to the original state.

Handling above the session level

Suppose that Sam wants to send a "good morning" e-mail to Estella. What exactly does the web do? We analyze it from the top down here to get a clear understanding that goes in the process.

Application Layer

User Sam creates a new e-mail message on the host computer (more usually in a browser), specifies the recIPient as Estella, and enters the message as "good morning". The software that sends and receives emails can be functionally divided into two categories one that is communication-related, and one that is not. For example, the part where user Sam enters "good morning" from the keyboard is a non-communication-related function, while the part where user Sam sends "Good Morning" to recIPient Estella is a communication-related function. Thus, "entering the contents of the e-mail message and send it to the target address" here is equivalent to the application layer.

From the moment the user enters what he wants to send and clicks the "send" button, the application layer protocol is processed. The protocol attaches a header (label) to the front end of the data to be transmitted. The first part identifies the message as "Good Morning" and the recIPient as "Estella ". This data with the first message is sent to host Estella and then the mail-receiving software on that host obtains the content through the "mail-receiving" function. After the application on the host, Estella receives the data sent by host Sam, the data header and the data body are analyzed And will be Saved it into a hard drive or other Non-volatile random-access memory, a storage device where data cannot be lost in a power outage, for processing. If the recIPient's mailbox space on host Estella is full and cannot receive new messages, an error is returned to the sender. The handling of such exceptions is also a problem that the application layer needs to solve.

Presentation Layer

The meaning of "presentation" in the presentation layer is "presentation" and "demonstration" Hence the focus on concrete representations of data (most famously, the way each computer allocates data in memory differently. Typically, large and small entities.). In addition, the use of different software applications will also lead to the performance of different forms of data. For example, some word processors create files that can only be opened and read by a specific version of the software provided by the word processor manufacturer.

So what can you do if you run into this kind of problem in your email? If user Sam and User Estella use exactly the same mail client software, they will be able to receive and read mail without similar problems. But this is unlikely to happen in real life. Getting all users to use the same client software in a cookie-cutter fashion is also a huge inconvenience for users (today, other devices, such as smartphones, besides pcs, are also connected to the Internet. How to make them read each other's communication data is becoming more and more important.

There are several ways to solve this kind of problem. The first is to use the presentation layer to convert data from "A computer specific data format" to "a standard network data format" before sending it out. After receiving the data, the receiving host restores the data in the network standard format to "the computer-specific data format", and then processes it accordingly.

In the previous example, the data was converted to a common standard format before being processed, allowing data consistency between heterogeneous models. This is what the presentation layer is for. That is to say, the presentation layer is a layer that transforms "the uniform network data format" and "the data format specific to a computer or a piece of software".

The text "Good Morning" in this example is converted to "unified network data format" according to its encoding format. Even if it is a simple stream of text that can be encoded in a variety of complex formats. Take Japanese, for example, EUC-JP, Shift, ISO-2022-JP, UTF-8, UTF-16, and many other encoding formats. If you cannot encode in a specific format. Then in the receiving end is the receIPt of mail may also be garbled (in real life when the receIPt and delivery of mail become garbled situation is not It's rare. This is usually because the presentation layer does not run in the expected encoding format or the encoding format is incorrectly set.).

In order to identify the encoding format, the presentation layer and the presentation layer will attach the header information, which will transfer the actual transmitted data to the next layer for processing.

Session Layer

Next, let's analyze how and how to efficiently interact with data between the session layers of the hosts on both sides of data transmission.

ASSUME THAT USER Sam has created five new e-mails ready to be sent to user Estella. These five messages can be sent in a variety of order. For example, you can establish a connection (a communication connection.) And then disconnect each time a message is sent. You can also send 5 emails to each other in a row once you've established a connection. You can even set up five connections at once and send five emails to each other at the same time. It is the primary responsibility of the session layer to decide which connection method to use.

The session layer, like the application or presentation layer, attaches a header or label to the front end of the data it receives before forwarding it to the next layer. These headers or tags contain information about the order in which the data is transmitted.

Handling Below the Transport Layer

So far, we have used examples to illustrate the general process of data written in the application layer is formatted and coded by the presentation layer and then sent out by the session layer tag. However, the session layer only manages when to establish a connection, when to send data and so on, and does not have the function of actually transferring data. It is the "Unsung Heroes" below the session layer that is really responsible for transmitting specific data over the network.

Transport Layer

Host a ensures communication with host Estella and is ready to send data. This process is called "making connections. ". With this communication connection, the e-mail sent by host Sam can reach host Estella, and the final data is retrieved by host Estella's Mail handler. In addition, it is necessary to disconnect the connection when the communication transmission is over.

As above, do the connect or disconnect processing (note here that the session layer is responsible for deciding when to connect and disconnect, while the transport layer does the actual connect and disconnect processing), the primary role of the transport layer is to create a logical communication connection between the two hosts. In addition, the transport layer verifies the arrival of the transmitted data at the destination address between computers on both sides of the communication and retransmits the data if it does not arrive.

For example, host a sends "Good Morning" data to host Estella. During that time, the data may be compromised for some reason Bad, or due to some kind of network exception that only part of the data reaches the destination address. Let's assume host Estella only received "Good Morning If it does not receive the "morning" part of the data, it will be notified of the fact that it did not receive the "morning" part of the data Host, Sam. Host Sam will be informed of this situation will be after the "good" resend to host Estella, and again to confirm whether the other side received.

It's like people saying, "Hey, what did you just say? " In everyday conversation, computer communication protocols aren't as Esoteric as you might think Its basic principle is closely connected with our daily life, much the same.

Thus, to ensure the reliability of data transmission is an important role in the transmission layer. To ensure reliability, a header is attached to the data to be transmitted at this layer to identify the hierarchical data. In practice, however, the processing of transferring data to the other end is done by the network layer.

Network Layer

The role of the network layer is to send data from the sending host to the receiving host in a network-to-network connected environment. Although there are many data links between the two end hosts, the ability to send data from host Sam to host Estella is also due to the network layer.

The Destination Address is critical when actually sending the data. This address is for Communication The unique ordinal number specified in the network. Think of it as a phone number that we use in our daily lives. Once the destination address is determined, the computer that sent the data to the destination address can be selected from a large number of computers. Based on this address, packets can be sent and processed at the network layer. With the address and network layer packet sending processing, data can be sent to any interconnecting device in the world. The network layer also sends the data and address information it receives from the upper layer to the data link layer below for later processing.

The RelationshIP Between the Transport and the Network Layer

Under the different network architecture, the network layer cannot guarantee the data accessibility sometimes. For example, in an IP protocol that is equivalent to the TCP / IP Network Layer, there is no guarantee that data will be sent to the opposite address. Therefore, the data transmission process data loss, the possibility of confusion and other issues will be greatly increased. In a network layer like this, where there are no reliable transmission requirements, the transport layer can be responsible for providing "proper transmission data handling. ". In TCP / IP, the network layer and the transport layer work together to ensure the reliable transmission of packets around the world.

The clearer the role and function of each layer, the simpler the specification of the protocol, implementation (that is, software coding specific protocols to make them work on a computer) will also make the task of implementing these specific protocols easier.

Data Link Layer, Physical Layer

Communication transmission is actually realized through physical transmission media. The purpose of the data link layer is to process data between these devices interconnected by a transmission medium. In the physical layer, 0 and 1 of the data are converted into voltage and pulse light for transmission to the physical transmission medium, while directly connected devices use the address for transmission. This address is called a Mac (Media Access Control, Media Access Control) address, and can also be called a physical or hardware address. The MAC address is used to identify devices connected to the same transmission medium. Therefore, in this hierarchy, the first part containing Mac address information is attached to the data forwarded from the network layer and sent to the network.

Both the network layer and the data link layer send the data to the receiver based on the destination address, but the network layer is responsible for sending the entire data to the final destination address, while the data link layer is responsible for sending only the data within a segment.

Processing of Host Estella Terminal

The processing flow on host Estella of the receiving end is just opposite to host Sam. IT starts from the physical layer and sends the received data to the previous layer for processing Thus, user Estella can finally use the mail client software on host Estella to receive the mail sent by user Sam, and can read the corresponding content as "good morning". as mentioned above, the reader can think of the functions of a communication network in layers. The protocol on each layer specifies the format of the data header in that layer and the order in which the header and the data are processed.

Classification of Transport Modes

Network and communication can be based on its data transmission methods for a variety of classification. There are many ways to categorize them, and here are a few of them.

Connectable Oriented vs. Connectionless Oriented

Sending data over the network can be divided into two types: connectionless-oriented and connectionless-oriented. connectionless-oriented includes Ethernet, IP, UDP, etc.. connectionless-oriented includes ATM, frame relay, TCP, etc.

Oriented Connected type

Oriented to connected type, in the case of sending data (in the case of connection-oriented data, the data at the sending end does not have to be sent in groups. we will see that TCP packets send data in connection-oriented fashion, circuit switching is also a connection-oriented fashion, but data is not limited to packet transmission.) A communication line needs to be connected between the transceiver hosts (the meaning of the connection may vary in different layered protocols. The connection in the data link layer refers to the connection of the physical, communication line. The transport layer is responsible for creating and managing logical connections.).

Facing connected is like people making a phone call. After typing in the phone number and dialing it out, only the other side can pick up the phone to make a real call. When the call is over, closing the phone is like cutting off the power. Therefore, in connection-oriented mode, it is necessary to establish and disconnect the connection before and after the communication transmission. If there is no communication with the other side, you can avoid sending unnecessary data.

Connectionless Oriented

Connectionless-oriented models do not require establishing and disconnecting connections. The sender is free to send data at any time (more often than not, packet switching is used for unlinked types. At this point, the data can be interpreted as packet data.). Conversely, the receiver never knows when and where it will receive the data. Therefore, in connectionless-oriented situations, the receiving end often needs to confirm that it has received the data.

It's like people going to the post office to mail a package. A postal clerk does not need to confirm that the recIPient's address actually exists, or that the recIPient can receive the package As long as the sender has a mailing address, he can handle the business of mailing parcels. Unlike telephone communication, connectionless communication does not require processing such as making a call or hanging up the phone. Instead, the sender is free to send the data it wants to transmit.

Therefore, in connectionless-oriented communication, there is no need to confirm the existence of the opposite end. The sender can send data out even if the receiver does not exist or cannot receive it.

Connection-Oriented and Connectionless-Oriented

The word "connection" in human society, equivalent to the meaning of "network". At this point, it refers to an acquaintance or a relationship between people. And facing connectionless, in fact, means no relationshIP at all.

In baseball and golf, one often hears the phrase "where to get the ball! ". This is, in fact, typical sender-side processing for connectionless communication. Some readers may consider connectionless-oriented communication to be a bit wonky. But for some special equipment, it is a very efficient method. Because this way can omit some established, complicated procedures so that the processing becomes simple, easy to produce some low-cost products, reduce the processing burden.

Circuit Switching and Packet Switching

At present, there are two kinds of network communication methods-circuit switching and packet switching. Circuit switching technology has a relatively long history, mainly used in the telephone network of the past. Packet switching technology is a relatively new form of communication, from the late 1960s began to be gradually recognized. This book focuses on the introduction of TCP / IP, it is the use of packet switching technology.

In circuit switching, the switch is mainly responsible for data transfer processing. The computer is first connected to the switch, and the connection between the switch and the switch is continued by a number of communication lines. Therefore, when sending data between computers, it is necessary to establish a communication circuit between the switch and the target host.

We call connecting circuits establishing connections. After the connection is established, the user can use the circuit until the connection is disconnected.

If a circuit is only used to connect the communication lines between two computers, it means that only the two computers need to communicate with each other, so the two computers can be exclusive lines of data transmission. But if there are multiple computers connected to a circuit, and these computers need to transfer data to each other, a new problem arises. Since one computer has exclusive access to the entire circuit while sending and receiving information, other computers have to wait until the computer has finished processing the data before they have a chance to use the circuit. And in the process, no one can predict when a computer's data transmission begins and ends. If the number of concurrent users exceeds the number of lines of communication between switches, communication is not possible at all.

To this end, people came up with a new method, that is, let the computer connected to the communication circuit to send the data to be divided into a number of packets, in a certain order and then sent separately. This is called packet switching. With packet switching, data is subdivided so that all computers can send and receive data at the same time, thus improving the utilization of communication lines. Since the addresses of the sender and receiver are written at the beginning of each packet, even if the same line serves multiple users simultaneously, it is also possible to make a clear distinction between the destination to which each packet is sent and the computer with which it is communicating.

In packet switching, a communication line is connected by a packet switch (router). The basic process of packet switching is that the sending computer sends the packet data to the router, which receives the packet data, caches it into its buffer, and then forwards it to the target computer. Therefore, packet switching also has another name: Cumulative switching.

Once the router receives the data, it caches it into a queue and sends it out one by one in a first-in, first-out order (sometimes, it gives priority to data with a more specific destination address).

In packet switching, there is usually only one communication line between computer and router and between router and router. So, this line is actually a shared line. In circuit switching, the speed of transmission between computers is constant. In packet switching, however, the speed of the communication line may be different. Depending on network congestion, the time it takes for the data to reach its destination can vary. In addition, when the buffer of the router is saturated or overflowed, it may even happen that packet data is lost and can not be sent to the opposite end.

Classification By Number of Receivers

In network communication, the communication can also be classified according to the number of the target address and its subsequent behavior. Such as broadcast, multicasting and so on is the product of this classification.

UNICAST

Literally, "Uni" means "1" and "Cast" means "Cast. ". The combination is one-on-one communication. An early example of unicast communication was the landline telephone.

BROADCAST

It literally means to play. So, it means sending a message from one host to all the other hosts that are connected to it.

A typical example of broadcast communication is the television broadcast, which sends the television signals together to non-specific multiple receivers.

In addition, we know that television signals generally have their own frequency bands. Television signals can be received only within the acceptable range of the corresponding frequency band. Similarly, computers that broadcast communications also have their broadcast range. Only a computer within this range can receive the corresponding broadcast message. This range is called the broadcast domain.

Multicast

Like Broadcasting, multicast sends messages to multiple receiving hosts. The difference is that multicast requires a certain set of hosts to be qualified as receivers. Multicasting is best exemplified by video conferencing, a type of remote conference that involves groups of people in different places. In this form, a message is sent from one host to a specific number of hosts. Video conferencing usually cannot be broadcast. Otherwise, there's no way of knowing who's there and where.

ANYCAST

Anycast is a method of communication in which one host is selected as a receiver. Although this approach is similar to multicast in that it targets a specific set of hosts, its behavior is different from that of multicast. Anycast communication. Select the host from the target host group that best meets the network conditions to send the message. Typically, the selected specific host will return a unicast signal, and then the sender host will only communicate with that host.

Anycast applications in real networks have DNS root domain name resolution servers

Address

In communication transmission, the sender and the receiver can be regarded as the communication subjects. They can all be identified by a message called "address". When people use a telephone, a telephone number is equivalent to an "address". When people choose to write a letter, an address plus a name is equivalent to an "address. ".

The real-life "address" is easier to understand, but in computer communications, the concept of this address appears to be more complex. Because in actual network communication, each layer of the protocol used by the address is not the same. For example, in TCP / IP Communications, MAC address, IP address, port number, and so on are used as address identifiers. Even in the application layer, an e-mail address can be used as the address of network communication.
the uniqueness of addresses.

If you want the address to play a role in communication, you first need to determine the main body of the communication. An address must explicitly represent a princIPal object. A communication subject with two identical addresses is not allowed to exist in the same communication network. This is the uniqueness of the address.

So far, the reader may have a question. As mentioned earlier, a communication subject with two identical addresses is not allowed to exist in the same communication network. This is understandable in UNICAST communications, where both ends of the communication are a single host. So for broadcast, multicast, and broadcast communication how to understand it?

Isn't the receiver assigned the same address? In fact, to some extent, this understanding has some rationality. In these communications, there may be more than one receiving device. For this reason, a unique address can be assigned to a group of communications composed of multiple devices, which can avoid ambiguity and explicitly receive objects.

Address Hierarchy

When the total number of addresses is not a lot of cases, with a unique address can be located between the main communication. However, when the total number of addresses is increasing, how to efficiently find out the target address of communication will become an important issue. For this reason, it is found that the address needs to be hierarchical as well as unique. In fact, in the use of telephone and mail communication process, the address hierarchy has long been a concept. For example, a telephone number contains a country area code and a domestic area code, and a correspondence address contains the name of the country, province, city, and district. It is this hierarchical classification that makes it possible to locate an address more quickly.

Both Mac address and IP address are unique in identifying a communication body, but the only the IP address is hierarchical.

Mac addresses are specified by the device's manufacturer for each NIC (Network Interface Card), also known as a Network

Card, which is used by computers to connect to the Internet.).
One can ensure the uniqueness of the MAC address through the
manufacturer's identification number, the manufacturer's
internal product number, and the generic product number.
However, it is impossible to determine which network cards
from which vendor are used in which location. Although the
MAC address has some level of information such as
manufacturer identification number, product number, and
general number, it doesn't do anything to find the address So it
doesn't count as a hierarchical address. Because of this, although
the MAC address is really responsible for the final
communication address, in the actual addressing process, the IP
address is essential.

So how do IP addresses achieve layering? On the one hand, an IP
address consists of a network number and a host number. Even
if the main communication IP address is different, if the host
number is different, the network number is the same, that they
are in the same network segment. In general, the hosts of the
same network segment also belong to the same department or
group. On the other hand, hosts with the same network number
are centralized in the organization, provider type, and
geographic distribution, which makes IP addressing very
convenient). That's why IP addresses are hierarchical.

In network transmission, each node will decide which network
card should send the packet according to the address

information of the packet data. To do this, each address refers to a list of outgoing interfaces. At this point, Mac addressing is the same as IP addressing. But the table referenced in the Mac addressing is called the address forwarding table. The reference in IP address is called the routing control table (currently, the forwarding table and the routing control table are not manually set up on each node in the network but are generated automatically by those nodes. Address forwarding tables are automatically generated based on self-study. The routing control table is automatically generated based on the routing protocol. The actual Mac address itself is recorded in the Mac address forwarding table, while the IP address recorded in the routing table is the centralized network number.

Network Components

Setting up a network environment involves a wide variety of cables and network equipment. Here only the hardware that connects the computer to the computer is described.

Communication Media and Data Links

Computer network refers to the computer and computer connected and composed of the network. So how are computers connected in the real world?

The computers are connected to each other by cables. There are many types of cables, including twisted pair, fiber optic cable, coaxial cable, serial cable, etc. A protocol and its network for communicating between directly connected devices based on data links (Datalink). To this end, there are a number of transmission medium corresponding. Different cable types are used. And the medium itself can be divided into radio waves, microwaves and other types of electromagnetic waves.

Transmission Rate and Throughput

In the process of data transmission, the physical speed at which data flows between two devices is called the transmission rate. In units of BPS (Bits Per Second). Strictly speaking, the flow rate of signals in various transmission media is constant. It's official. Therefore, even if the data link transmission rate is not the same, there will be no transmission speed fast or slow situation (because the speed of transmission for light and current is constant.) High transmission rate does not mean how fast per unit data flow and Refers to the amount of data transmitted per unit time.

In the case of road traffic in our lives, low-speed data links are like too few lanes for many cars to pass through at once The situation. In contrast, a high-speed data link is a road with multiple lanes, allowing more vehicles to travel at once. The transmission rate is also known as Bandwidth. The greater the bandwidth, the greater the network capacity.

In addition, the actual transfer rate between hosts is called throughput. The units are the same as the bandwidth, BPS (Bits Per Second). Throughput is a term that measures not only bandwidth, but also the CPU capacity of the host, congestion on the network, and the share of data fields in the message (not including the header, only the data fields themselves).

The Connection Between Network Devices

Interconnectivity between network devices needs to follow some kind of "law" of norms and industry standards. This is critical to setting up an online environment. If each different vendor uses its own transport medium and protocol when producing various network devices, those devices will not be able to connect to other vendors' devices or networks. To this end, people have developed a unified agreement and specifications. Every manufacturer must produce corresponding network equipment in strict accordance with the specifications, otherwise it will lead to its own products cannot be compatible with other network equipment, or prone to failure and so on.

However, norm-setting is often a long-term process, in this process of technological transition, people will inevitably encounter some "compatibility" problems. This is especially true in the early days of new technologies such as ATM, Gigabit Ethernet, and Wireless Lan. Problems often occur when network devices from different vendors connect to each other. This has improved over time but is still not 100% compatible.

Therefore, when building the actual network, not only should pay attention to the specification parameters of each product, but also should understand their compatibility And more attention should be paid to the actual long-term use of these products in the course of the performance indicators (performance indicators good technology is also known as "mature technology. ". It refers to the market and users over a period of time test, accumulated a considerable amount of practical experience of technology. If you use a new product that doesn't work well without proper research, the consequences can be dire.

Network Card

Any computer connected to the network must use a network card (the full name is the network interface card). The network interface card (Nic) is an integrated device that connects Lan functions. Sometimes it is integrated into the computer's motherboard, or it can be inserted into an expansion slot separately Use. Network Information Center (Network Information Center) is sometimes called a Network adapter, Network card, or LAN card.

Recently, many product catalogs have added the parameter "built-in Lan port", note that more and more computers in the factory settings with Ethernet (Ethernet)1000BASE-T or 100BASE-TX port (computer and external connection interface known as computer port.). A computer that does not have a NIC configured needs to have at least one external socket to plug into the NIC if it wants to connect to Ethernet. By the PC Card standard PCMCIA (Personal Computer Memory Card International Association) unified specifications. Or CardBus compressed flash Memory and USB plug a piece later connected.

Repeaters

Repeater (Repeater) is a device that extends the network at the physical level, layer 1 of the OSI model. The electrical or optical signals from the cable are adjusted and amplified by the waveform of the repeater and transmitted to another cable.

In general, the two ends of the repeater are connected to the same communication medium, but some repeaters can also complete the transfer between different media. For example, signals can be adjusted between the coaxial cable and optical cable. In this case, however, the repeater is simply responsible for replacing the signal between the 0 and 1-bit streams, not for determining whether the data is in error. At the same time, it is only responsible for converting electrical signals into optical signals Therefore, it can not be forwarded between media with different transmission speeds (one 100 Mbps Ethernet and another 10 Mbps Ethernet cannot be connected with a repeater. Connecting two networks of different speeds require devices such as bridges or routers.).

Network extensions via repeaters are not infinitely long in distance. For example, a 10Mbps Ethernet can be connected in segments with up to four repeaters, while a 100Mbps Ethernet can be connected to up to two repeaters.

Some repeaters can provide multIPle port services. This type of repeater is called a relay hub or hub. Therefore, a can also be considered A MULTI-PORT REPEATER Each port can be a repeater.

Bridge / Layer 2 SWITCH

A Bridge is a device that connects two networks at layer 2 of the OSI model, the data link layer. It recognizes data frames in the data link layer (similar to packet data, but more commonly referred to as frames in the data link layer). And temporarily store these data frames in memory, the regenerated signal is then forwarded as a new frame to another connected segment of the network. In addition, data can also be represented in TCP. Because of the ability to store these frames, the bridge is able to connect 10BASE-T and 100BASE-TX data links with completely different transmission rates and does not limit the number of links.

A bit in the data frame of a data link is called FCS (CRC Cyclic Redundancy Check Check) to verify the bit in the data frame. This kind of CRC is used to check whether a data frame has been damaged by the noise that sometimes causes the data signal to get weaker and weaker in the transmission To verify that the data has reached its destination correctly. Bridges Discard corrupted data by checking the values in this field to avoid sending it to other segments. In addition, the bridge can control network traffic (the number of datagrams transmitted over the network) through address self-learning mechanism and filtering function

By address, I mean the Mac address, hardware address, physical address, and adapter address, which is the specific address assigned to the NIC on the network.

When host a communicates with host B, only a data frame can be sent to host A. The bridge determines whether a frame needs to be forwarded based on the address self-learning mechanism.

This is the function of Layer 2(data link layer) of the OSI reference model. For this reason, bridges are sometimes referred to as layer 2 switches (L2 switches).

Some bridges, called self-learning bridges, are able to determine whether or not to forward data packets to adjacent segments. This type of bridge remembers the Mac address of all the frames it forwards and stores them in its own memory table. From this, you can determine which network segment contains devices that hold which MAC addresses.

A Hub (a Bridge-enabled Hub called a switching Hub, and a repeater-only Hub called a Hub), often used in networks such as Ethernet, is now essentially a Network bridge Hub. Each port connected to the cable in the switching hub provides a bridge-like function.

Router / Layer 3 switch

A router is a device that connects two networks at layer 3 of the OSI model, the network level, and forwards packet packets. The bridge is processed according to the physical address (Mac address), while the router / Layer 3 switch is processed according to the IP address. Thus, the network layer address in TCP / IP becomes the IP address.

A router can connect to different data links. For example, connect two Ethernet networks, or connect one Ethernet to an FDDI. Nowadays, the broadband router that people use to connect to the Internet in their home or office is also a kind of router.

The router also shares the network load (since the router splits the data link, the broadcast message at the data link layer will not continue to propagate.), some routers even have some network security features. Therefore, the router plays a very important role in connecting the network and the network equipment.

4 ~ 7 layer switch

Layer 4 ~ 7 switches handle data from the transport layer to the application layer in the OSI model. If the TCP / IP layer model is used (for more details about the TCP / IP Layer Model), layer 4-7 switches analyze the sending and receiving data based on the transport layer of TCP and the application layer above it And do certain things with it.

For example, for an enterprise-level Web site with a high level of concurrent traffic (a server or group of servers connected to the Internet as specified by the URL. At present, according to information content can be divided into game sites, resource download sites and Web sites and other types One server is not enough to meet the front-end access requirements, and multIPle servers are usually set up to share. These servers typically have only one entry address for front-end access (the enterprise only opens a unified access URL to the end user for user convenience). In order to distribute front-end access to multiple servers in the background via the same URL, a load balancer can be added to the front end of these servers. This load balancer is one of the 4-7 layer switches (in addition to load balancing via DNS. By configuring multiple IP addresses with the same name, each customer querying the name gets one of the addresses, enabling different clients to access different servers. This approach is also known as the reuse DNS technique.).

In addition, in actual communications, people want to give priority to communication requests that require more timeliness, such as voice calls, when the network is more congested Slow down the processing of communications requests, such as email or data forwarding, where a slight delay doesn't hurt. This process is called bandwidth control and is one of the important functions of layer 4 ~ 7 switches.

In addition, there are many applications of layer 4 ~ 7 switch. Examples include WAN accelerators, special application access accelerators, and firewalls that prevent illegal access on the Internet.

Gateway

A gateway is a device in the OSI reference model that is responsible for converting and forwarding data from the transport layer to the application layer (by convention, a router behaves like a "gateway"). But "gateways" in this book are limited to devices or components in the OSI reference model that convert protocols at each layer above the transport layer.). Like layer 4 ~ 7 switches, it processes data at the transport layer and above, but the gateway not only forwards the data but also converts it. It usually uses a presentation layer or application layer gateway Two protocols which cannot communicate with each other directly are translated, and the communication between them is realized finally.

A very typical example is the switching service between Internet mail and Mobile Mail. Mobile mail can sometimes be incompatible with Internet mail because of the "e-mail protocol" differences between the presentation layer and the application layer.

So why do computers and phones connected to the Internet send e-mails to each other? There is a gateway between the Internet and the phone. The gateway is responsible for reading various protocols, converting them reasonably one by one, and then forwarding the corresponding data. This allows computers and mobile phones to send e-mails to each other, even if different e-mail protocols are used.

In addition, when using the WWW (World Wide Web), Proxy Server is sometimes used to control network traffic and for security reasons. This proxy server is also a type of gateway, called an application gateway. With the proxy server, there is no direct communication between the client and the server on the network layer. Instead, data and access are controlled and processed from the transport layer to the application layer. A firewall is a communication through the gateway, for different applications to improve security products.

Chapter 4: Advanced Networking

In this chapter, we will expand our knowledge further about reference models and learn in detail about TCP protocol.

Physical layer

When it comes to the "physical layer" of network architecture, the first thing to know is what it does. Compared with other layers, the "physical layer " includes more technologies and procedures because of the types of transmission media, physical interfaces and their communication protocols (that is, "communication protocols") But its main functions are relatively simple, including.

(1) Building a Data Path

"Data Path" is a complete data transmission channel, can be a section of physical media, can also be connected by a number of physical media. A complete data transfer, including the activation of the physical connection, transfer of data, termination of the physical connection three major stages. The so-called "activation of physical connection", is no matter how many pieces of physical media involved, in the communication between the two data terminal equipment must be connected to form a continuous data transmission channel above.

(2) Transparent Transmission

There are many types of transmission media available in the physical layer (such as different types of coaxial cable, twisted pair and optical fiber, et c.), each supported by corresponding communication protocols and standards This determines that different computer networks may have different "paths. ". In addition to repairing these different "paths", the physical layer also ensures that these different "paths" can be "connected" to form paths that eventually carry the bitstream to the "physical layer" on the opposite end the purpose of which is then submitted to the data link layer.

To achieve these functions, the physical layer needs to have the function of shielding different transmission media types and communication protocols, so that the parties communicating on the network can only see that there is a " road" available Regardless of the specific "material" and related standards used to build these "roads" , this is the "transparent transport" function of the physical layer.

(3) Transmission of Data

No matter which layer of the network architecture initiates the communication, the final data has to be transmitted through the lowest "physical layer", which is the only physical channel of the network communication. But the unit of transmission for the "physical layer" is the bit (bit, or "bit", where a Binary 0 or 1 in the data represents a bit). The basic function of "physical layer" is to transmit data in the order of bit stream to the physical layer of the receiver through the physical layer interface and transmission medium.

(4) Data Coding

In order to transmit the data efficiently and reliably on the "physical layer" , the most important thing is to ensure that the data bit stream can pass through the corresponding "channel". This involves the "physical layer" of data encoding functions because different transmission media support different types of data encoding (such as zero-return code, non-zero-return Code, Manchester Code, differential Manchester Code, etc.).

(5) Data Transmission Management

The "physical layer" also has some functions of data transmission management, such as data transmission flow control, error control, activation and release of physical lines, etc.

Datalink Layer

The data link layer is included directly or indirectly in computer network architectures (the functionality of the data link layer in the TCP / IP Protocol Architecture is included in the network access layer). The data link layer and the physical layer below it are essentially the same, that is, they are used to build a channel for network communication and access, only the physical layer builds a physical channel the data link layer builds logical channels that are really used for data transmission. Because of this, in the TCP / IP Protocol Architecture which is widely used on the Internet, the physical layer and the data link layer are divided into the network access layer.

The data link layer is located in the lower layer of the "network layer" (called the interconnect layer in the TCP / IP Protocol Architecture) of the network architecture. So one of its basic functions is to provide transparent, reliable data transfer services to the network layer (in a computer network architecture, the next layer serves the next layer next to the one above). "transparent" means that there are no restrictions on the content, format, or encoding of the data being transmitted at the data link layer This means that some control characters that are intended for special purposes (which are described later in this chapter) can be transmitted as normal data so that the receiver does not mistake them for control characters; Reliable transmission enables data to be transmitted from the sending end to the destination end of the data link without error. Overall, the main functions of the data link layer (in this case, the LLC sublayer) are four: Data Link Management, encapsulation into frames, transparent transmission, and error control.

Network Layer

If we compare the physical layer and the data link layer to intra-city traffic, the network layer described in this chapter can be compared to a transit station, airport, or dock that connects different urban traffic. Just as a transit station, airport or dock can transport passengers from another city to the next stop or to a local destination, the network layer can transfer data from other networks to the next network or to a destination node in this network. When the source and the destination are located in different networks, direct communication is not feasible, then it needs to be solved by the network layer.

Network Layer (called interconnect layer in TCP / IP Architecture) is a very important layer in network architecture, and it is also a very complicated layer in technology It not only solves the problem of route and protocol identification, but also solves the problem of network congestion by route selection strategy, so as to improve the reliability of network communication. The network layer is concerned with routing packets from the source along the network path to the destination. To achieve this goal, the network layer must know the topology of the communication subnet and choose the proper path in the topology. At the same time, the network layer must choose the routing path carefully to avoid the situation that some communication lines and routers are overloaded while others are idle.

The physical layer and the data link layer introduced earlier in this book construct the communication lines within the LAN, which are equivalent to the traffic lines within a city. The network layer described in this chapter is the node used to connect different local area network lines, located at the edge of the different network, is equivalent to the edge of the city, used to connect different urban transit points.

The network layer is the third layer in the OSI reference model (corresponding to the second layer in the TCP / IP Protocol Architecture, the interconnect layer), which is between the transport layer and the data link layer. Generally speaking, the main role of the network layer is to achieve the transparent transmission of data between the two network systems, including routing, congestion control, and Internet interconnection. The network layer is the lowest layer of the end-to-end (that is, between the network and the network) network communication. It is responsible for the connection to the resource subnet above it (Osi / RM reference model transport layer and above four layers) and is the most complex and critical layer of the network communication-oriented lower three layers of the OSI / RM reference model.

The network layer is the product of the development of the computer network, but it is not the product of a computer network. In the early days of computer networks, there was basically a separate local area network, and we know that In the LAN, the communication link constructed by the physical layer and the data link layer can be used to realize the communication access among the users, so there is no need for other layers, including the network layer. Moreover, at that time, the application of computer network was limited, and there was no need to communicate with each other among local area networks, so these local area networks did not need to be connected with each other. But with the popularization and development of computer networks, it is increasingly found that it is very necessary to connect these isolated local area networks one by one to form a larger computer network so that the role of computer networks can be more obvious Enable more people to share server and hardware resources. This involves the interconnection of computer networks.

So why such a network layer? In fact, the reason is very simple, because different networks have different network layer protocols and address specifications, if users in one network cannot identify the other network communication protocols and address specifications, you can't transfer data from one network to another. Just as different cities have different traffic laws and regulations, belong to different traffic police systems, and do not allow random traffic in and out of the city, different networks have different design specifications, belong to different organizations to manage, and must be authorized and special protocols are responsible for communication between the networks.

Usually a computer network is a management boundary, generally belongs to a specific company, by a specific manager responsible. Therefore, when the interconnection of computer networks is carried out, two aspects should be considered at the same time: one is to authorize users to visit each other's network s and share their resources; the other is to maintain the original independence of the management of each computer network So the problem cannot be solved simply by pulling a cable (this does not solve the problem of management independence) . In fact, in many environments, it is not possible for a typical business to connect two computer networks located in different cities or even different countries via a tether.

The main function of the network layer is to route packets from the source node to the destination node, and in most computer networks, packet switching is used Datagram packets go through multIPle hops (that is, how many routers) to reach their destination.

Routing

The routing function is actually a packet switching path selection behavior, is a basic function of the network layer. Routing functions are similar to the way we choose the best (note that "best" doesn't mean the fastest, it's a combination) to travel or transport goods.

There can be multiple routes for sending such a letter. Different routes require different ways of mailing, different length of route and time of mailing, and of course, different transportation costs. The final choice of route should be considered in terms of overall mailing cost, mailing time and reliability of the post office. Routing is the same, it has to consider a number of factors, such as line length, channel bandwidth, line stability, the cost of the port through. Different routing algorithms take into account different factors.

Routing is the act of transferring information from the source node to the destination node via the network. Simply speaking, Routing means that three layers of devices receive packets from one interface and Orient them according to the destination address of the packet And forward it to another interface. But at least one intermediate node needs to be encountered in this routing path, and that is the devices that provide routing functions, such as routers and layer 3 switches. The main difference between routing and bridging is that bridging occurs at layer 2(link layer) of the OSI reference protocol, connecting different segments of the same network or subnetwork, and routing occurs at Layer 3 (network layer) Connected to a different network or subnet.

The realization of the routing function depends on the routing table in the router or three-layer switch. There are two kinds of Routing: Static Routing and Dynamic Routing.

Static routing is something we often need to configure, especially in small Lens, because it is relatively simple to configure and manage

Static routing is feasible for small and infrequently changing networks, such as local area networks. However, for larger Wan, because the topology is more complex and the network structure may change frequently, the static routing is no longer suitable, and the dynamic routing is more flexible and automatic.

One of the most important features of dynamic routing is that the routers included in a route in the network simultaneously start a dynamic routing protocol, after notifying the networks to which they are directly connected These routers will automatically generate routing table entries between the networks to which the routers are directly connected, and administrators do not have to create each one manually. This is the most convenient and simple routing option for larger networks.

IP addresses

The most important protocol of Osi / Rm Network layer and TCP / IP interconnect layer is IP protocol, which is in the transition period of IPV4 and IPv6 So this chapter will be the two versions of the IP address and related knowledge of the system

IPv4 uses 32-bit (4-byte) addresses, so there are 4294967296(2^{32}) addresses in the entire address space or nearly 4.3 billion addresses. However, some of these addresses are reserved for special purposes, such as Lan private addresses (about 18 million addresses) and multicast addresses (about 27 million addresses), in this way can be directly used in the wide area network, the number of public networks IP address routing is even less.

To understand what a subnet mask is, one must first understand the composition of an IPV4 address. The Internet is made up of many small networks, each network has many hosts, thus forming a hierarchical structure. In the design of IPV4 address, each IP address is divided into two parts: a Network ID and host ID, so as to facilitate the addressing operation of IPV4 address. So how many bits are the network ID and host ID of an IPV4 address? If it is not specified, it is not known which bits in the IPV4 address represent the network ID and which represent the host ID at the time of addressing, which is realized by the subnet mask mentioned here.

In the whole network architecture, the bottom three layers of OSI / RM seven-layer model are called communication subnet-oriented layers, which are responsible for the establishment of the communication channel, and the transport layer and above are called resource-oriented subnet-oriented Layers Responsible for data communication between Terminal Systems. There is also a way to divide the "transmission layer" and the following three layers into a communication-oriented layer, in general, responsible for the establishment of communication channels and data transmission The "session layer" , "presentation layer" and " application layer" , which do not contain any data transfer function, are collectively called application-oriented layers.

Application Layer

The application layer is the highest layer of the OSI / Rm and TCP / IP architectures. It provides services directly to users by using the services provided by the following layers. It is the interface or interface between a computer network and users. Just like the services provided by other layers, the service functions of the application layer are realized by specific communication protocols.

Used by users on a daily basis Such as Web Service, e-mail service, DNS (domain name service), DHCP (automatic IP address assignment service), file transfer service, remote login service, etc. With the popularization and development of Internet application, a variety of new network application services emerge in endlessly. This chapter only introduces some of the most commonly used services in TCP / IP Network.

The application layer in TCP / IP architecture solves the common problems of TCP / IP network applications, including the supporting protocols and application services related to network applications. The supporting protocols include domain name service system (DNS), dynamic host configuration protocol (DHCP), simple network management protocol (SNMP) and so on Typical application services include Web browsing service, E-mail service, file transfer access service, remote login service, etc. In addition, there are some protocols related to these typical network application services This includes Hypertext Transfer Protocol, Simple Mail Transfer Protocol, File Transfer Protocol, simple File Transfer Protocol, and remote login (Telnet).

The most popular and frequently used Web application is the World Wide Web (WWW) service or Web service. The core application layer Protocol for Web Services is HTTP (Hypertext Transfer Protocol), which can also be viewed as the "hero behind the Hypertext Transfer Protocol" of Web Services.

The Background and History of TCP / IP

At present, TCP / IP Protocol is the most famous and widely used in the field of a computer network. So how did TCP / IP become so widespread in such a short time? Some think it's because PC operating systems such as Windows and MAC OS support TCPIP. While this is true to a certain extent, it is not the root cause of the popularity of TCPIP. In fact, around the entire computer industry at that time, the whole society formed a popular trend to support TCP / IP, so that various computer manufacturers have to adapt to this change and continue to produce products to support TCP / IP. Today, you can hardly find an operating system that doesn't support TCPIP on the market.

In a literal sense, one might think that TCP / IP refers to both TCP and IP protocols. In practice, it does sometimes refer to these two agreements. However, in many cases, it is only the use of IP communication must be used in the group of protocols collectively. Specifically, IP or ICMP, TCP or UDP, TELNET or FTP, and HTTP are TCP / IP Protocols. They have a close relationship with TCP or IP and are an integral part of the Internet. The term TCP / IP generally refers to these protocols, and therefore, TCP / IP is sometimes referred to as the Internet Protocol Suite (the Group of protocols that make up the Internet Protocol Suite).

The standardization process of TCP / IP Protocol Is Different From other standardization processes, which has two characteristics: one is openness, the other is practicality, that is, whether the standardized protocol can be used in practice.

First, openness is because the TCP / IP Protocol is discussed by the IETF, and the IETF itself is an organization that allows anyone to participate in the discussion. Here, people typically have daily discussions in the form of e-mail groups, which can be subscribed to by anyone at any time.

Secondly, in the process of standardization of TCP / IP, the specification of a protocol itself is no longer so important, but the first task is to realize the technology that can realize communication. No wonder some people quIPped that "TCP / IP is simply to develop the program first, then write specifications. ".

Although that's a bit of an exaggeration, however, TCP / IP does take into account the feasibility of implementing a protocol when developing a protocol specification (implementation: the development of programs and hardware that enable a computing device to perform certain actions or behaviors as expected by the protocol). And while the final specifications for a protocol are in place, some of these protocols already exist in certain devices and can communicate.

To this end, as soon as the general specification of a protocol is determined in TCP / IP, people will experiment with the communication between multiple devices that have implemented the protocol, and once they find something wrong, they can continue to discuss it in the IEFT Modify programs, protocols, or corresponding documents in a timely manner. After so many discussions, experiments, and studies, a protocol specification is finally born. Therefore, the TCP / IP Protocol is always very practical.

However, for those protocols that were not found to be problematic due to the limitations of the experimental environment, improvements will continue at a later stage. The reason OSI is not as popular as TCP / IP, the main reasons were the failure to formulate feasible agreements as early as possible, the failure to propose agreements to deal with rapid technological innovation and the failure to implement late-stage improvement programs in a timely manner
TCP / IP is the most widely used protocol in a computer network. Knowledge of TCP / IP is critical for those who want to build networks, build networks, manage networks, design and build network devices, and even do network device programming.

At the bottom of TCP / IP is the hardware responsible for data transmission. This hardware is equivalent to a physical layer device such as an Ethernet or telephone line. There has been no consistent definition of what it is. Because as long as people on the physical level of the use of different transmission media (such as the use of network lines or wireless), the network bandwidth, reliability, security, delay, and so on will be different, and in these areas, there are no established indicators. In a word, TCP / IP Protocol is proposed on the premise that the interconnect devices can communicate with each other.

The network interface layer (sometimes called the network communication layer by combining the network interface layer with the hardware layer) uses the data link layer in the Ethernet to communicate, so it belongs to the interface layer. That is, think of it as the "driver" that makes the NIC work Prologue doesn't matter. A driver is a software that bridges the gap between the operating system and the hardware. PerIPheral devices or extension cards are not immediately available by plugging them directly into a computer or its expansion slot and need to be supported by a corresponding driver. For example, a new NIC network card, not only the need for hardware but also the need for software to really put into use. As a result, people often need to install drivers on top of the operating system in order to use additional hardware. (There are also many plug-and-play devices because the computer's operating system already has drivers built into the network card, rather than no drivers.).

The Internet layer uses the IP protocol, which is equivalent to layer 3 of the OSI model. A number of IP packets forwarded based on the IP Address. In addition, all hosts and routers connected to the Internet must implement IP functionality. Other network devices that connect to the Internet (such as bridges, repeaters, or hubs) do not necessarily have to perform IP or TCP functions (sometimes they also need to have IP, TCP functions in order to monitor and manage bridges, repeaters, hubs, and the like)

IP is a protocol that transmits packets across a network, enabling the entire Internet to receive data. The IP protocol enables data to be sent to the other side of the Earth During this time it uses the IP address as the identity of the host (all devices connected to the IP network must have their own unique identification number in order to identify the specific device. Packet data is sent to the opposite end based on the IP address.). IP also implies the function of the Data Link Layer. Through IP, the hosts can communicate with each other regardless of the underlying data link.

Although IP is also a packet switching protocol, it does not have a retransmission mechanism. Packets do not resend even if they do not arrive on the end host. Therefore, it belongs to the non-reliable transport protocol.

When an exception occurs on the way to the IP packet and the destination address can not be reached, a notification of the exception is sent to the sender. ICMP is designed for this purpose. It is also sometimes used to diagnose the health of the network.

A protocol for resolving a physical address (MAC address) from the IP address of a packet.

The primary function of the transport layer is to enable communication between applications. Inside a computer, usually, several programs are running at the same time. To this end, it is necessary to distinguish which programs are communicating with which programs. What identifies these applications is the port number.

TCP is a connection-oriented transport layer. It can ensure that communication between the two communication hosts can reach. TCP can correctly handle the transmission process in the loss of packets, transmission order out of order and other abnormal cases. In addition, TCP can effectively utilize bandwidth and alleviate network congestion.

However, in order to establish and disconnect the connection, sometimes it needs at least 7 times to send and receive the packet, leading to the waste of network traffic. In addition, in order to improve the utilization of the network, TCP protocol defines various complex specifications, which is not conducive to the use of video conferencing (audio, video data set) and other occasions

UDP, unlike TCP, is a connectionless oriented transport layer. UDP does not care whether the other end is actually receiving the transmitted data, and if it needs to check whether the other end is receiving packet data, or whether the other end is connected to the network, it needs to be implemented in the application. UDP is often used in multimedia fields such as packet data less or multicast, broadcast communication, and video communication.

In the TCP / IP Layer, the functions of the session layer, presentation layer, and application layer in the OSI reference model are integrated into the application sequential implementation. These functions are sometimes implemented by a single program or by multiple programs. Therefore, a closer look at the application functions of TCP / IP reveals that it implements not only the application layer of the OSI model but also the session layer and presentation layer.

The architecture of TCP / IP application mostly belongs to the Client / Server Model. The program that provides the service is called the server, and the program that receives the service is called the client. In this mode of communication, the service provider is predeployed to the host, waiting to receive requests that customers may send at any time.

The client can send a request to the server at any time. Sometimes the server may handle the exception, overload, and so on when the client can wait a moment to reissue a request.

WWW (worldwide Web, a specification for reading data on the Internet. Sometimes also called Web, WWW or W3.) Can Be said to be the Internet can be so popular an important driving force. Users in a type of browser called the Web Browser (often referred to simply as the browser). Microsoft's Internet Explorer and Mozilla Foundation's Firefox are all browsers. They are already widely used.) With the help of a mouse and keyboard, you can surf the web freely and easily. That means that a single click of the mouse on a remote server will render all kinds of information to the browser. The browser can display text, pictures, animation, and other information, but also play sound and run programs.

The Protocol used for communication between the Browser and the server is HTTP (Hypertext Transfer Protocol). The primary format of the data transferred is HTML (Hypertext Markup Language). HTTP in the WWW belongs to the OSI application layer protocol, while HTML belongs to the presentation layer protocol.

E-mail actually means sending letters on the Internet. With email, no matter how far away a person is, just connect to each other. You can send e-mails to each other over the Internet. The Protocol used to send e-Mail is called SMTP (Simple Mail Transfer Protocol).

Initially, people could only send e-mails in text format (consisting only of text messages. Japanese originally could only send 7- bit JIS encoded text.). But now, the format of an e-mail message is defined by MIME (a specification for the format of mail data that is widely used on the Internet. It can also be used in WWW and web forums. For more details on this point, You can send sounds, pictures, all kinds of information. You can even change the size and color of the message text (some functions may not be fully displayed due to the limitations of the mail-receiving software). The MIME mentioned here belongs to Layer 6 of the OSI reference model, the presentation layer.

File transfer (FTP)

A file transfer is the transfer of a file stored on another computer's hard drive to a local hard drive or the transfer of a file from a local hard drive to another machine's hard drive. The protocol used in this process is called FTP (File Transfer Protocol). FTP has been in use for a long time (the use of HTTP with the WWW for file transfer has been increasing recently) you can choose between the binary or text mode of the transfer. (text-based file transfers between systems such as Windows, MacOS, or Unix change line breaks automatically. This is also part of the presentation layer.). Two TCP connections are established when a file transfer is made in FTP, these are the control connections used to make transmission requests and the data connections used to actually transmit data (the control management of these two connections is a function of the session layer).

Remote Login (TELNET and SSH)

Remote login is the ability to log on to a remote computer, allowing programs on that computer to run. Teletext (short for TELetypewriter NETwork, sometimes referred to as the default protocol) and SSH (short for Secure Shell) are two common protocols for remote login over TCP / IP Networks. There are many other protocols that allow remote Logins, such as the R command for login in BSD UNIX systems and the x protocol in x Window System.

Network Management (SNMP)

When Network Management in TCP / IP, SNMP (Simple Network Management Protocol) Protocol is used. Hosts, bridges, routers, etc. that are managed using SNMP are called SNMP agents, and the segment that is managed is called a Manager. SNMP is the protocol used by this Manager and Agent.

In the agent side of SNMP, the information of network interface, communication data, abnormal data, and device temperature are stored. This Information can be accessed through the Management Information Base, also known as a network-permeable structural variable. Therefore, in the network management of TCP / IP, SNMP belongs to Application Protocol, MIB belongs to Presentation Layer Protocol.

The larger and more complex a network is, the more it needs to be managed effectively. SNMP allows administrators to check network congestion in a timely manner, to detect failures early, and to collect the necessary information for future network expansion.

How are TCP / IP Transmitted over a Medium?

This section describes the flow of data processing from the application layer to the physical media when using TCP / IP.

Packet Header

In each hierarchy, a header is attached to the data being sent, which contains the necessary information for the layer, such as the destination address to be sent and protocol-related information. Typically, the information provided for the protocol is the header of the package, and the content to be sent is data.

The data packet transmitted in the network consists of two parts: one part is the first part used by the protocol, and the other part is the data transmitted from the upper layer. The structure of the header is defined in detail by the specification of the protocol. For example, the domain that identifies the upper layer protocol should start with which bit of the package, how to compute the checksum and insert which bit of the package, and so on. If the two computers communicating with each other are different in identifying the serial number of the protocol and calculating the checksum, they can not communicate at all.

Therefore, at the beginning of the packet, it clearly indicates how the protocol should read the data. Conversely, by looking at the header, you will be able to understand the information necessary for the protocol and what to process. Therefore, looking at the header of the package is like looking at the specification of the protocol.

No wonder people say the first one is like the face of protocol sending packets

Suppose a sends an e-mail to b saying, "Good Morning". In TCP / IP Communication, it is an e-mail from one computer A to another computer B. Let's use this example to explain the process of TCP / IP Communication.

Application Processing

Launch the application to create a new message, fill out the recipient's mailbox, then enter the message content "good morning" by keyboard, mouse click on the "send" button can start the TCP / IP Communication. First, there is coding in the application. For example, Japanese e-mail is encoded using ISO-2022-JP or UTF-8. These codes correspond to Osi's presentation layer functions.

After the code conversion, the actual message may not be sent immediately, because some mail software has the ability to send more than one message at a time there may also be the ability for users to click the "receive mail" button before receiving new mail. Such administrative functions as when to establish a communication connection and when to send data are, in a broad sense, functions of the OSI reference model at the session layer.

The application uses the TCP connection to send data by establishing the TCP connection at the moment the message is sent. The process is to send the application data to the next layer of TCP, and then do the actual forwarding processing.

The Processing of TCP MODULE

TCP is responsible for establishing connections, sending data, and disconnecting according to the application's instructions (which are equivalent to the session layer in the OSI reference model.). TCP provides reliable transmission of data from the application layer to the opposite end.

In order to realize this function of TCP, we need to attach a TCP header to the front end of the application layer data. The TCP header includes the source and destination port numbers (to identify applications on the sending host and the receiving host) , the serial number (which part of the packet to send is the data) , and the Checksum (Check Sum)(to verify that the data is read properly)(to determine whether the data is corrupted) . The packet attached to the TCP header is then sent to the IP.

The Processing of IP Module

IP takes the TCP header and TCP data from TCP as its own data and adds its own IP header to the front end of the TCP header. Thus, the IP header in an IP packet is followed by the TCP header, followed by the application header and the data itself. The IP header contains the receiver IP address and the sender IP address. Immediately following the IP header is the information used to determine whether the following data is TCP or UDP.

After the IP packet is generated, the reference routing control table decides which route or host to accept the IP packet. The IP packet is then sent to the driver that connects to these routers or host network interfaces to actually send the data. If the MAC Address on the receiving end is not known, an ARP (Address Resolution Protocol) lookup is available. As long as we know the MAC address of the opposite end, we can give the MAC address and IP address to the Ethernet driver to realize data transmission.

The Processing of Network Interface (Ethernet Driver)
The IP packet that comes over from IP is nothing more than data to the Ethernet driver. This data is attached to the Ethernet header and sent for processing. The Ethernet header contains the Mac address of the receiver, the Mac address of the sender, and the Mac address of the marked Ethernet type. Ethernet data protocol. The Ethernet packet generated from the above information will be transmitted to the receiving end through the physical layer. The FCS (Frame Check Sequence) in the send processing is computed by the hardware and added to the end of the package. The purpose of the FCS is to determine whether a packet has been corrupted by noise.

Network Interface (Ethernet driver) Processing
After the host receives the Ethernet packet, it first finds the MAC address from the Ethernet packet header to determine whether the packet is sent to itself. Discard data if it is not sent to its own

packet (many NIC products can be set to not discard data even if it is not sent to its own packet. This can be used to monitor network traffic.).

If you receive a packet that happens to be sent to you, look for the type field in the header of the Ethernet packet to determine the type of data being transmitted by the Ethernet protocol. In this case, the data type is obviously an IP packet, so it passes the data to the processing IP subroutine, and if it's not IP but some other protocol such as Arp, it passes the data to the ARP handler. In summary, if the type field at the head of the Ethernet packet contains an unrecognized protocol type, the data is discarded.

The Processing of IP Module
The IP module receives the first and subsequent portions of the IP packet and does similar processing. If you determine that the IP address in the header matches your own IP address, you can receive the data and look up the protocol at the next level. If the upper layer is TCP, the portion after the header of the IP packet is passed to TCP; if UDP, the portion after the header of the IP packet is passed to UDP. In the case of Router, the receiver address is often not their own address, at this point, the need to use the routing control table, in the investigation should be sent to the host or router after forwarding data.

The Processing of TCP Module

In the TCP module, the CHECKSUM is first calculated to determine whether the data is corrupted. Then check to see if the data is being received by serial number. Finally, check the port number to determine the specific application. After the data is received, the receiver sends an "acknowledgment receIPt" to the sender. If the return message fails to reach the sender, the sender thinks the receiver is not receiving the data and keeps sending it back and forth.

When the data is received in its entirety, it is passed to the application identified by the port number.

Application Processing

The receiver application receives the data sent by the sender directly. By parsing the data, you can know the recipient location of a message the address is B's address. If host B does not have a mailbox for B, then host B returns an error message to the sender that says "No to this address".

But in this case, host B happens to have B's inbox on it, so host B and recIPient B can receive the body of the e-mail. The message will be saved to the hard drive of the computer. If the save also works, the receiver will return a "process normal" receipt to the sender. On the other hand, if the disk is full and the message is not saved successfully, a "handle exception" receIPt is sent back to the sender.

Thus, user B can use the mail client on host B to receive and read the e-mail sent by the user a -- "Good morning".

SNS (Social Network Service), called Social networking and is a Service for instant sharing and instant messaging to specific contacts within a circle. As described in the previous e-mail communication process, the process of sending or receiving SNS messages with a mobile terminal can also be analyzed. First, because mobile phones, smartphones, tablets and so on are communicating with packet data, the specific IP address is set by the carrier at the moment they are loaded into a battery and turned on. When you start an application on a mobile phone, you connect to the specified server, and the accumulated information from the server is sent to the mobile terminal after the user name and password are verified, and the terminal displays the specific content.

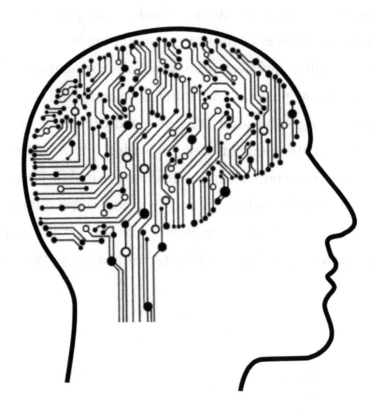

Chapter 5: Machine Learning & Computer Networking

Before going to discuss the use of machine learning in Computer networking there is a need to know in detail about machine learning, deep learning, and Artificial intelligence.

First of all, people are often confused with definitions. Artificial intelligence is a branch of computer science that makes computers work to think like a human. Machine learning is a branch of Artificial intelligence where computers can be made to think like humans with a lot of data given. Deep learning is a branch of Machine learning which uses complex algorithms for text, image and face recognition.

All these three technologies are interlinked and can help computer networks to work better and can act as an intrusion detection system. We will now know briefly about machine learning, artificial intelligence and deep learning for better use of this book content.

In the 1950s and 1960s, with the birth of the computer, artificial intelligence quietly emerged in university labs. Marked by the Turing test proposed by the Alan Turing, the mathematical proof system, Knowledge-based systems, expert systems and other landmark technology and application of artificial intelligence suddenly set off the first wave of researchers.

But at that time, whether it is the computing speed of computers or related programming and algorithm theory, is far from enough to support the development of artificial intelligence needs. In 1951, for example, the Alan Turing, a pioneer in computer science and artificial intelligence, published a paper version of a chess program, but computers of that time could not perform such complex calculations. Like the Explorer Wild China, there's a big difference between setting foot on a new continent for the first time and actually making it flourish. As a result, from the late 1960s, enthusiasm for AI quickly waned among both professional researchers and the general public.

From the 1980s to the 1990s, that's when I invented speaker-independent continuous speech recognition at Carnegie Mellon University and applied it to Apple Computer Systems -- a golden age for AI researchers and product developers. Traditional semiotic-based techniques have been abandoned by me and other contemporary researchers, and statistical-model-based techniques have emerged, making considerable progress in areas such as speech recognition and machine translation Artificial neural networks have also begun to make headway in applications such as pattern recognition, and the 1997 triumph of the deep blue computer over the Human Garry Kasparov has given ordinary people a run for their money.

But the technological advances of that era were not good enough to exceed the psychological expectations of intelligent machines. In the case of speech recognition, the statistical model, while a big step forward for speech recognition technology, is not yet good enough for the average person to accept. At the time, the speech recognition APP I developed at apple was used more for presentations and promotions, with limited practical value. On the whole, that wave of artificial intelligence still has strong academic research and scientific experiment color, although aroused public enthusiasm, more like a bubble before hitting bottom It is far from being in line with the business model and the needs of the masses.

Around 2010, to be exact, since 2006, as deep learning technologies mature, computer computing speeds increase dramatically, and, of course, the wealth of vast amounts of data accumulated in the Internet Age Artificial intelligence is on a different path to a renaissance.

Psychologically, there is a psychological threshold for people to accept something new, just as it is for people to feel an external stimulus. The intensity of external stimuli (such as sound, light, and electricity) is too small for people to feel anything at all; only the intensity of external stimuli exceeds the minimum amount of stimuli a person can perceive People have definite feelings such as "hearing voices" and "seeing things". This minimum amount of stimulus, known psychologically as an absolute threshold, causes a person to perceive and react.

That's exactly what's happening with artificial intelligence. Still, take image recognition. In the early days of artificial intelligence, if a computer program claimed it could recognize a face in a picture, it was only about 50 percent accurate the average person would see the program as a toy, not as intelligent. As technology advances, and as face recognition algorithms improve their accuracy to 80 percent or even close to 90 percent, researchers know that this is not an easy step to take, but the results are still hard for ordinary people to accept Because one out of every five faces is misidentified, this is obviously not practical -- One might say the program is clever, but one would never think it was smart enough to replace the human eye. Only when the accuracy of the computer in face recognition is very close to or even higher than that of ordinary people, the security system will use the computer to replace the human security to complete the identification work. In other words, for face recognition applications, approaching or exceeding the level of the average person is the "absolute threshold" that we care about.

So, when we say "AI is here, " we mean that ai or deep learning can really solve real problems. In Machine Vision, speech recognition, data mining, automatic driving, and other application scenarios, artificial intelligence has continuously broken through the psychological threshold that people can accept, and for the first time in the industrial level "landing" to play and create real value.

How Does Computer Learn?

What kind of laws does the computer come up with? It depends on what kind of machine learning algorithm we use.

There is an algorithm very simple, imitation is a child learning to read the idea. Parents and teachers may have the experience that when children begin to learn to read, for example, when we teach them to distinguish "one" from "two" from "three", we tell them that the word written in a stroke is "one" Two strokes make two characters, three strokes make three characters. This rule is easy to remember and easy to use. However, when it comes to learning new characters, this rule may not work. For example, "mouth" is also three strokes, but it is not three strokes. We usually tell the children that the box is the mouth and the row is the three. The pattern thickens, but the number of words is still rising. Soon, the children found that "field" is also a box, but it is not "mouth. We will tell the children at this time, the box has a "Ten" is the "field". After that, we will probably tell the children, "field" above the head is "by", below the head is "a", above and below is "Shen". Many children are in such a step-by-step enrichment of the characteristics of the law under the guidance of slowly learn their own summary of the law, their own remember new Chinese characters, and then learn thousands of Chinese characters.

Deep Learning

Deep learning is such a machine learning approach that is flexible in its expressiveness while allowing the computer to experiment until it finally gets close to its goal. In essence, deep learning is not fundamentally different from the traditional machine learning methods described above but is intended to distinguish different classes of objects in high dimensional space based on their characteristics. But the expressive power of deep learning is vastly different from that of traditional machine learning.

In simple terms, deep learning is the process of taking what a computer is trying to learn and putting that data into a complex, multi-level data processing network (deep neural network) Then check that the resulting data processed by the network meets the requirements -- if it does, keep the network as the target model, and if it does not, adjust the network parameters Veronica Guerin again and again Until the output meets the requirements.

Suppose the data to be processed by deep learning is the "flow" of information, and the deep learning network is a huge network of pipes and valves. The entrance of the network is a number of pipe openings, and the exit of the network is also a number of pipe openings. The water network has many layers, each layer has many can control the flow of the water flow direction and flow control valve. According to the needs of different tasks, the number of layers and the number of regulating valves in each layer of the water pipe network can have different combinations. For Complex tasks, the total number of regulator valves can be in the thousands or more. In a water pipe network, each control valve in each layer is connected to all control valves in the next layer through a water pipe, forming a front-to-back fully connected layer-by-layer flow system (this is a basic case where different deep learning models differ in the way pipes are installed and connected).

Side note: There are already some visualization tools out there that can help us "see" deep learning on a large scale. For example, Google's famous deep learning framework, Tensor Flow, provides a web version of a gadget that maps out the real-time features of the entire web as it performs deep learning operations using easy to understand diagrams.

Finally, it is important to note that the above concept of deep learning deliberately avoids mathematical formulas and mathematical arguments, and this method of popularizing deep learning with water networks is only suitable for the general public. For Math and computer science professionals, this description is incomplete and inaccurate. The flow control valve analogy is not mathematically equivalent to the weight adjustment associated with each neuron in a deep neural network. The cost function, gradient descent, backpropagation and other important concepts of deep learning algorithm are neglected in the whole description of the water pipe network.

Should professionals learn deep learning, or should they start with a professional tutorial?

Now let us know with a few examples of how machine learning algorithms can be used in computer networking.

Computer networking is a strange field and is often vulnerable to scammers and hackers who try to destroy the otherwise good game into a cruel one with viruses, ransoms, Trojans and certain other weird stuff that can make networks suffer and lose a lot of money, energy and time. Machine learning can be used in intrusion detection systems to secure the network environment. Below we will discuss a few algorithms and its effect on network security.

1. K-Nearest Algorithm
It is a famous machine learning algorithm which can be used to detect network shells and spam content in the network.

2. Decision Tree Algorithm
Decision tree algorithm can be used to detect abnormal operations in the network with a lot of sample data it had collected.

3. Random Forest Algorithm
Random forest machine learning algorithm can be effectively used to detect abnormal operations in the network and can also be used to detect brute force attacks via FTP.

4. Naïve Bayes Algorithm

Naïve Bayes algorithm can be used to detect network shells and DDOS attacks in a computer network.

5. Logistic Regression Algorithm

By using logistic regression algorithm there are huge chances of stopping java overflow attacks that occur often from malicious hackers.

6. Support Vector Machine

Support Vector machine is famous for its detection abilities of Botnets and it can also be used to detect XSS vulnerability in web-based applications.

7. K-Means and DB-Scan Algorithm

Both of these algorithms can be used to detect all types of attacks that occur on computers with an accurate precision rate.

And there are certain deep learning algorithms that can help you detect your employees all the time for any error they may do. By using machine learning and deep learning methods in computer networks we can make networks a lot secure. Machine learning with computer networks has a lot of potential in the coming days.

Conclusion

Thank you for making it through to the end of *Networking for beginners*, let's hope it was informative and able to provide you with all of the tools you need to achieve your goals whatever they may be.

The next step is to learn more about computer networking from various advanced textbooks. Hope you have learned a lot with this module. For further exploration of computer networks try to look at different hardware you encounter in your life.

This module follows up with a layman introduction to machine learning and artificial intelligence. You can check it to improve your expertise in the field.

Just for a quick overview of the material we have seen. We have learned about definition, history, and basics of networking with a thorough overview of a network with a lot of examples. Then we discussed network protocols in detail. And in the end, we discussed Artificial intelligence and machine learning with respect to Computer Networking.

Finally, if you found this book useful in any way, a review on Amazon is always appreciated!

www.ingramcontent.com/pod-product-compliance
Lightning Source LLC
Chambersburg PA
CBHW071206050326
40689CB00011B/2261